STRAIGHT ANSWERS TO PEOPLE PROBLEMS

The Briefcase Books Series

Managing Stress: Keeping Calm Under Fire
Barbara J Braham

Business Negotiating Basics
Peter Economy

Straight Answers to People Problems
Fred E Jandt

Empowering Employees Through Delegation
Robert B Nelson

The Presentation Primer: Getting Your Point Across
Robert B Nelson
Jennifer Wallick

Listen for Success: A Guide to Effective Listening
Arthur K Robertson

STRAIGHT ANSWERS TO PEOPLE PROBLEMS

Fred E Jandt

IRWIN
Professional Publishing
Burr Ridge, Illinois
New York, New York

Sponsoring editor: Cynthia A. Zigmund
Project editor: Amy E. Lund
Production manager: Laurie Kersch
Designer: Larry J. Cope
Cover designer: Tim Kaage
Compositor: Wm. C. Brown Communications, Inc.
Typeface: 11/13 Palatino
Printer: Book Press, Inc.

Library of Congress Cataloging-in-Publication Data

Jandt, Fred Edmund.
    Straight answers to people problems / Fred E. Jandt.
        p.   cm. — (The Briefcase books series)
    Includes bibliographical references and index.
    ISBN 1-55623-849-5   0-7863-0201-1 (Paperback)
    1. Communication in management. 2. Management. I. Title
II. Series
HD30.3.J36 1994
658.3—dc20   93-30800

Printed in the United States of America
    2   3   4   5   6   7   8   9   0   BP   0   9   8   7   6   5   4

Preface

If you picked up this book because of its title, my guess is there's a specific work-related people problem on your mind. You probably don't want to read a long, involved theoretical book; you want some guidelines and a fast answer, so you can redirect your energies back to the job. That's what this book is for.

Let me tell you briefly how it came to be written. I conduct management training seminars in different aspects of business communication—particularly negotiation and customer service. But no matter the subject of the training program, there's always a line of people after the seminar who want to ask my advice on a particular problem back at work.

If you have attended one of my seminars, you know I base my coaching on personal experience as a manager in professional and academic organizations and as a small business owner/manager.

This book, then, is a collection of fast, direct answers to the most common people problems managers like you have asked me about. Its purpose is to give you those few minutes of coaching you need to deal quickly with that situation yourself.

The reader most likely to profit from this book is the person who has been able to make use of management training seminars—particularly team leaders, supervisors, new managers, first-line managers, human resource managers, and small business operators and owners: people who can find themselves faced with a troublesome people problem for which they need just a bit of direction, so they can then deal with it effectively.

The book is organized into 24 commonly faced problems. Each section provides background information, examples, and suggestions for dealing with a problem. Each section can easily be read in a few minutes. You can flip to your most pressing question or read the book from beginning to end. Reading the whole book might just help you avoid some of these problems in the future!

Managers have told me that one use they've found for the book is to give a copy to associates when they're experiencing a problem or when they're new to the job. In any case, I recommend keeping the book handy. You know that solving one people problem doesn't prevent others from occurring in the future!

Acknowledgments

In 1984, I was asked by Paula Farley Green, the editor of *Modern Dentalab* (at the time a Huethig publication, later published by Stevens Publishing Corporation) to write a regular column on communication for dental laboratory managers. The columns were developed under the editorial direction of Paula Farley Green, Eileen Doherty, Brenda Spears Tacker, and David Mantooth and form the bases of some of the chapters in this book. I gratefully acknowledge their cooperation.

Fred E Jandt

Briefcase Books—Series Introduction

Research shows that people who buy business books (1) want books that can be read quickly, perhaps on a plane trip, commuting on a train, or overnight, and (2) feel their time and money were well spent if they get two or three useful insights or techniques for improving their professional skills or helping them with a current problem at work.

Briefcase Books were designed to meet these two criteria. They focus on necessary skills and problem areas, and include real-world examples from practicing managers and professionals. Inside these books you'll find useful, practical information and techniques in a straightforward, concise, and easy-to-read format.

This book and others like it in the Briefcase Books series can quickly give you insights and answers regarding your current needs and problems. And they are useful references for future situations and problems.

If you find this book or any other in this series to be of value, please share it with your co-workers. With tens of thousands of new books published each year, any book that can simplify the growing complexities in managing others needs to be circulated as widely as possible.

Robert B Nelson
Series Editor

Foreword

My mission in life has been to be a conveyor of simple truths. It is for that reason that I'm pleased to be able to introduce the Briefcase Books Series, which seeks to provide simple, practical, and direct answers to the most common problems managers face on a daily basis.

It has been my experience that, in the field of business, common sense is not common practice. So it is refreshing to find a series of books that glorifies common sense in dealing with people in the workplace.

Take the skill of listening. We all know that it is important to listen, yet how many of us actually do it well? I believe that it would be rare to find 1 in 100 managers who is truly a good listener. Most people focus on what they are going to say next when someone else is talking. They seldom, if ever, think to check what they thought they heard to make sure it is accurate. And they seldom acknowledge or attempt to deal with emotions when they occur in speaking with someone at work. These are basic errors in the use of this basic skill. And regardless of how much education or experience you have, you should know how to listen.

But how much training have you had on the topic of listening? Have you ever had a course on the topic? Have you ever tested your ability to listen? Have you ever discussed with others how you could listen better with greater comprehension and respect? Probably not. Even though this fundamental interpersonal skill could cripple the most talented individual if she is not good at it.

Fortunately, listening is just one of the fundamental skills singled out for its own volume in the Briefcase Books Series. Other include books on making presentations, negotiating, problem solving, and handling stress. And other volumes are planned even as I write this.

The Briefcase Books Series focuses on those basic skills that managers must master to excel at work. Whether you are new to managing or are a seasoned manager, you'll find these books of value in obtaining useful insights and fundamental knowledge you can use for your entire career.

Ken Blanchard
Co-author
The One Minute Manager

Contents

I

COMMUNICATION SKILLS

1. Improving Listening Skills

Problem:

How can I remember more of what people say?

Answers:

Set listening goals.
Assume an active role.

BACKGROUND

Many of us can remember playing the children's game of telephone: One person whispers something to another person. That person, in turn, whispers the same message to a third person. And that person to a fourth and so on. The last person says aloud what he heard. Usually, the results are hilarious, since many facts are dropped and others are distorted—sometimes beyond recognition.

Communication scholar Larry L Barker[1] has identified several common listening problems:

1. *Preparing our next statement or question while the other person is talking.* I believe this is our most common listening problem. Most of us are poor listeners, because when another person is talking we're thinking about what we are going to say next, rather than listening to what the person is saying.

As a manager you must correct any bad listening habits.

2. *Wasting the advantages of "thought speed" over "speech speed."* It is said that we think at a rate of 400 words per minute, while speakers talk at a rate of only 200 words per minute. This difference leads some of us to allow our minds to wander off, rather than use the time to evaluate what we're hearing.

3. *Viewing the information as uninteresting.* Sometimes we don't listen, because we don't believe what the other person is saying is interesting.

4. *Attending to how the speaker looks or talks.* Unusual dress or unusual speech patterns or dialects may distract our attention from what is being said.

5. *Getting emotionally involved.* When we become ego-involved in something the person has said, we may focus on our emotions and not the information.

6. *Allowing emotionally laden words to interfere with listening.* A single word can be distracting when we have an emotional response to that word and stop listening.

7. *Permitting personal prejudices to impair comprehension and understanding.* A person's use of racial slurs makes listening difficult for most of us.

8. *Listening only for what we think we need.* It is so easy to listen only for the information we think we need, thus ignoring other critical information the person gives.

9. *Trying to make what the person says fit our needs.* Sometimes we distort what the person says, so we get what we think we need.

10. *Tolerating or failing to adjust to distractions.* If for some reason, the environment becomes distracting, some change is in order. You can't stop the city from working on the street outside your window, but you can move away from the window.

11. *Faking attention.* There are times when outside thoughts come to mind, and you cannot force yourself to listen to the other person. For example, "What was I supposed to bring home from the grocery store?" "Did I forget to return that call?"

12. *Listening only to what is easy to understand.* As listeners we can avoid difficult listening. If the person is relating a complicated incident in painstaking detail, it can be difficult to listen.

These 12 listening problems are not exhaustive nor mutually exclusive. They do, however, represent, some of the more common bad listening habits.

EXAMPLES

Barker has also prepared a list of suggestions for improving listening. Many of the suggestions are, in essence, positive statements of the common listening problems listed earlier.

1. *Practice listening.* It has been found that applying good listening skills in difficult listening situations improves listening in normal circumstances. Practice listening for factual information at religious services, in television interviews and news broadcasts, at boring meetings, and so forth.

> *Most of us are poor listeners, because when the other person is talking we're thinking about what we are going to say next . . .*

2. *Build your vocabulary.* Not only expand your vocabulary in general but recognize that specialized areas have specialized vocabularies. For example, publishers use words and phrases such as *first serial rights, subsidiary rights, copyright, packaging, byline, kill fee, advances,* and *foreign rights.*

3. *Determine the personal value of the topic for you.* Remind yourself that listening is a very real and important part of your job.

4. *Be mentally and physically prepared to listen.* Our listening skills are related to our physical and mental condition. If you are tired, your listening performance is reduced. You have to be physically and mentally in shape for best results.

5. *Think about the content in advance when possible.* This suggestion is based on learning research that has demonstrated that if you are somewhat familiar with a topic before you attempt to learn about it, then learning takes place more efficiently and is longer lasting.

6. *Listen for main points.* Listen for the facts that, in your experience, are critical. It is not necessary to remember the extraneous material.

7. *Concentrate—don't let your thoughts wander.* Focus on what the other person is saying.

8. *Be flexible in your views.* Approach all situations with an open mind.

9. *Compensate for emotion-rousing words.* Remember, some words can arouse a reaction that interferes with your

listening. It is necessary to suppress your emotional reaction by recognizing that the word does not have the same associations for the other person as it does for you.

10. *Compensate for ideas and actions to which you react emotionally.* When the speaker uses words or brings up ideas and actions that trigger an emotional reaction that will interfere with your listening comprehension, there are ways to compensate:

- Defer judgment. Learn to withhold judgment until you have heard all the person has to say.
- Empathize. Take the other person's point of view to identify with their ideas and actions. While different than your own, the other person's ideas and actions may be logical or right from her perspective.
- Place your own feelings in perspective. Culture, family, and education have molded each of us into a unique person with unique beliefs and values. While another person's views may be different from our own, they represent his background and are not necessarily right or wrong.

Listening is critical to being a good manager. Your listening can be improved, but you have to work on it.

SUGGESTIONS

As a manager you must correct any bad listening habits. The first step is *motivation.* One has to truly want to be a more effective listener because to do so takes conscious effort. Becoming a better listener requires *setting goals* and *assuming an active role in listening.*

Setting listening goals means predetermining what you are listening for. With many employees, we need to listen for information. This has been labeled *discriminative listening,* since the objectives are understanding and remembering.

This involves understanding the meaning of words from context, understanding the relationship of details to main points, understanding the sequence of events, listening for details, listening with the intent to ask probe questions, and listening to take notes. Concentrated listening involves listening to comprehend everything the employee says.

Assuming an active role in listening means working at listening. This can be contrasted with passive listening, which is barely more than hearing. Passive listening involves receiving the sounds and letting them evoke thoughts. To assume an active role in listening is to do more than react to sound. It means working consciously to meet our listening objectives of understanding and remembering. Taking notes to record the information is one way of assuming an active role.

FOR MORE INFORMATION

Check in the business section of your local bookstore for books on listening. Here's one:

Bone, D. *The Business of Listening.* Los Altos, CA: Crisp Publications, 1988.

2.   Conducting Meetings

Problem:

How can I run better staff meetings?

Answers:

First decide if a meeting is really necessary.

Be sure everyone understands the purpose and agenda.

Use a systematic meeting management system.

BACKGROUND

Perhaps no statement causes more dread than, We need to have a staff meeting. Some of us believe that meetings are inefficient and a waste of time or that attending a meeting is not legitimate work. Many people recall the saying, A camel is a horse designed in a meeting. Yet, although we may dread meetings, we still have them.

According to San Francisco-based consultants Michael Doyle and David Straus, a meeting is "any time three or more people work together face-to-face to plan, solve problems, make decisions, present information, or give feedback. There are 11 million meetings a day in the United States alone."[1] So, not only do we have meetings, we have a lot of them.

Organizations spend 7 to 15 percent of their personnel budget, 35 percent of middle management's time, and 60 percent of top management's time in meetings.

SUGGESTIONS

Staff meetings can be productive, even legitimate work. However, the first question to ask is whether or not a staff meeting is even appropriate. Groups do some things well and other things poorly.

Keep in mind what can and cannot be accomplished in a staff meeting. Groups are not good at organizing large amounts of data, synthesizing lots of ideas, or writing reports. Individuals organize and write reports more efficiently than groups do. Groups are good for brainstorming, exchanging opinions and information, surfacing problems, discussing issues, and making final decisions.

Be sure that everyone understands the agenda and their individual roles and responsibilities. Remember what most people assume a meeting should be like: it should be held in the manager's office and everyone should sit around a table. The manager should develop the agenda, sit (and remain seated) at the head of the table, and run the meeting by Robert's Rules of Order.

When I'm attending a staff meeting of questionable productivity, I have a habit of calculating the personnel cost of that meeting to the organization. For example, assume that one manager and seven employees make an average salary of $35,000 a year plus benefits of 40 percent. In this example, a one-hour staff meeting costs the business owner over $192—without coffee. The question is, Did I get $192 worth of legitimate work from that staff meeting?

EXAMPLES

Whether or not you use Doyle and Straus's interaction method, which is explained later in this chapter, here are some tips for better staff meetings:

1. Decide whether or not a meeting is appropriate. Keep in mind that having a meeting just because it's scheduled is neither productive nor team building. A meeting is appropriate when:

- You want an issue clarified.
- You have concerns you want to share with your group as a whole.
- You want information from your group.
- You want to involve your group in solving a problem or making a decision.
- Your group wants a meeting.

A meeting is *not* appropriate when:

- The subject is trivial.
- You can communicate better by telephone.

- You have to deal with personnel issues, such as hiring, firing, and negotiating salaries.
- The subject matter is so confidential that it can't be shared with some group members.
- There is inadequate data or poor preparation.
- You have already made the decisions on the proposed meeting's topic.

2. Plan ahead to have an effective meeting. This can be accomplished by doing the following:

- Make the purpose clear.
- Prepare a clear agenda.
- Make sure all employees know what is expected of them in the meeting.
- Verify that everyone is well prepared.
- Make sure the room and seating arrangement support the meeting's purpose.
- Make the decision-making procedures explicit ahead of time.

I have seen a manager's displeasure with a meeting that she thought was to *announce* a policy change and the others in the room thought was to *discuss* a proposed policy change. That manager thought she was the decision maker who had called the group meeting to explain a decision that had already been made. The others thought she was one of a group of decision makers who had called the group meeting to solicit input. Certainly this was a case of misunderstanding the agenda and roles.

One method for conducting meetings suggested by Doyle and Straus is called the *interaction method*. They point out that when a manager tries to use a staff meeting to generate and share ideas, the manager is trying to do too much—to run the meeting, participate and encourage others to participate, remain neutral, and be the chief decision maker.

Their two suggestions are to assign group members to the roles of facilitator and recorder and use a group memory.

A facilitator can be anyone—a member of the group or not. The facilitator is the group's servant who keeps the members focused on the group's task. The job of facilitator can be rotated from member to member each meeting. When acting as a facilitator, a person no longer evaluates nor contributes ideas. The facilitator runs the group by focusing the group on one task at a time and by encouraging everyone to participate.

To employ group memory, first have the group sit facing a chalkboard or a blank wall with a large sheet of white paper taped to it. The group recorder writes notes as the discussion progresses. The group's work is immediately visible to the group members.

Using Doyle and Straus's interaction method permits the manager to be an active participant without having to carry all the burdens of directing the meeting.

Finally, even if you conduct a smoothly run meeting, there is still one job left—the follow-up. Nothing kills employees' enthusiasm for meetings more than a lack of follow-through. Be sure accountability is made clear, that is, who is expected to do what by when. After all, there's at least $192 at stake.

FOR MORE INFORMATION

Check in the business section of your local bookstore for books on meetings. Here are some:

Burleson, C W. *Effective Meetings: The Complete Guide.* New York, NY: Wiley, 1990.

Doyle, M and D Straus. *How to Make Meetings Work.* 1st ed. New York, NY: Wyden Books, 1976.

Frank, M O. *How to Run a Successful Meeting—in Half the Time.* New York, NY: Simon and Schuster, 1989.

3.   The Grapevine

Problem:

How can I deal with rumors and gossip?

Answers:

Establish and regularly use varied communication media to build management's credibility as an information source.

In a crisis, make special efforts to keep people informed.

Disprove rumors early.

BACKGROUND

"Did you hear the latest?" Who among us hasn't been involved in gossip and rumor? Who among us doesn't wish business was free from gossip and rumor?

Gossip is small talk with or without factual basis. Gossip deals with the personal affairs of individuals.

Gossiping has been called a "feminine" pastime. The Yiddish word for rumormonger is *yenta*, which is defined as a female gossip and is a sexist slur when uttered by a man. This old stereotype just isn't true. What is usually called *gossip* when done by women is just called *shop talk* or *shooting the breeze* when done by men. In reality, gossiping isn't limited to either sex.

Emotional needs, attitudes, and values may explain who gossips. Some people gossip, but most are "dead-enders"—people who hear gossip but never pass it on. It may be that gossips are less popular. In some cases gossiping may be a way of exchanging information for attention from another person.

Rumor is information neither substantiated nor refuted. Rumors deal with events and issues of great, real importance to the people involved.

Reasons for spreading rumors may be different. Whereas gossiping may be motivated by ego and status needs, rumors seem most often to be a way to provide meaning, clarification, and closure in ambiguous conditions.

And, rumors can cost us. If nothing else, they cost us the nonproductive time employees spend spreading rumors. I'm sure Procter & Gamble worked hard to put an end to the persistent rumor that it was affiliated with the Church of Satan—a rumor which seems to have originated out of a misinterpretation of a trademark.

EXAMPLES

In a widely known book, *The Psychology of Rumor,* Gordon W Allport and Leo Postman[1] argue that rumors are likely to occur when events are important and news is lacking or ambiguous. The key ingredients are importance and ambiguity.

Stated in a positive way, rumors can be said to be a form of group problem solving. Our minds strive to eliminate chaos and uncertainty, so we piece together information as best we can. The reason rumors circulate is that they explain things and relieve the tensions of uncertainty. Rumors are a way to cope with the uncertainties of life.

As James Fenimore Cooper wrote in *Miles Wallingford,* "Everybody says it, and what everybody says must be true."

The classic illustration is the 1938 rumor of an invasion of Earth by creatures from the planet Mars. The rumor originated in a CBS radio dramatization by Orson Welles of H G Wells's novel *The War of the Worlds.* The broadcast came within a month of the Munich crisis. For weeks the American people had been listening closely to their radios for on-the-spot news coverage. This, combined with the technical realism of the broadcast, created a panic that swept across the United States.

With one of my graduate students, I studied a rumor at an industrial plant in upstate New York.[2] The plant employed some 400 hourly employees. A nearby metropolitan newspaper had published an article indicating that the plant would be shut down for four weeks, that an estimated 50 to 60 hourly employees would be laid off, and that production of one of the major product lines would be cut by 50 percent.

Management had informed the employees about the loss of the new product line. Nevertheless, the long-term implications of the cutback in production and subsequent pending layoffs were not fully explained. The workers were threatened by a situation over which they had little control and about which they received severely limited information.

Our study showed that nearly all the rumors heard were repeated. Most of the rumors were spread while employees were on lunch breaks or were actually at work. Few rumors were repeated outside the plant. Generally, if a person considered a rumor accurate, it was repeated. Most of the rumors dealt with the layoffs and the possibility of a complete closing or relocation of the facility. Interestingly, regardless of their age, individuals with more seniority appeared to be more anxious than employees with less seniority.

SUGGESTIONS

A rumor can be said to have three general stages: birth, adventure, and death.

1. Birth. Why does anyone start a rumor? Some are started with sinister motives. Most may be attempts to provide information to explain an anxious situation.

2. Adventures. Rumormongering takes more than one person: one person's needs are satisfied in the telling, and the recipient's needs are satisfied in the listening. And with sufficient importance and ambiguity, a rumor can spread throughout a whole group.

As rumors are spread by word of mouth, the rumor is subject to considerable change as it passes from individual to individual. The children's game of telephone illustrates what can happen to the original story:

- Fewer words are used and fewer details are mentioned as the rumor travels. Initially there is a sharp decline in length and detail, and then the rumor stays about the same, because there isn't that much detail left.

- There is a sharpening, or emphasis, on a limited number of details.
- The rumor becomes adapted to conform to the views, prejudices, and values of the people passing it on.

3. Death. Some rumors are stillborn; others grow to maturity and die a natural death because of disproof or because the situation changes and the underlying tensions have dissipated. People may get tired of them and stop talking and thinking about them.

Some rumors never die. The speculations surrounding President John F Kennedy's assassination will probably be a part of our society for many, many years.

In organizations, the formal relationships (the organizational chart) represent the formal communication channels, whereas social relationships give rise to the informal communication channels used for rumors.

Keith Davis, a professor of management at Arizona State University, has studied these informal channels—commonly called the *grapevine*.[3] We know some things about any organization's grapevine.

1. The grapevine is more effective and faster than the formal lines of communication for the messages it carries.

2. Some people don't pass the message on. Others tell several people, and some people are not told.

3. The grapevine will always be with us. Attempts to suppress it in one place may only cause it to appear elsewhere.

Davis described grapevines as expressions of the healthy, natural human motivation to communicate. Our businesses and organizations can be fertile ground for rumors because the preconditions, importance and ambiguity, are there.

For most of us, the business or organization is our only source of income—so it's very important.

One of the basic outcomes of organizing is structure—a hierarchy. Structure, or specialization of jobs, restricts free flow of information. To be efficient, not everyone in an organization can know everything that's going on.

So with importance and ambiguity built into our business and organizations, we can expect rumors. The grapevine will always be there, but we can control the spread of rumors:

1. Do not discount the importance of the routine sources of information about the business. Newsletters and bulletin boards establish management as a reliable information source.

2. In a crisis or highly ambiguous situation, make a special effort to keep people informed. Issue as much news as quickly as possible to fill any vacuum of ambiguity with reliable information.

3. Specific outbreaks should be dealt with early. Experience shows that prompt, unequivocal disproof is the most effective way of stopping a rumor. Disprove the false rumor early, before people have had time to conclude that the rumor is true.

FOR MORE INFORMATION

Business communication writers haven't focused as much on rumors and gossip as have the social psychologists. So the best references are in that area:

Rosnow, R L. *Rumor and Gossip: The Social Psychology of Hearsay.* New York, NY: Elsevier, 1976.

4. Encouraging Upward Communication

Problem:

How can I get my employees to come forward with suggestions?

Answers:

Use a wide variety of techniques from informal conversation to opinion surveys.

Be responsive to what you get.

BACKGROUND

Every organizational hierarchy presents a dilemma. If everyone in the business were to be kept totally informed about every aspect of the business in detail, the organization just might collapse from information overload, and no work would get done.

So one important purpose of organization is to limit the flow of information to reach those individuals who need it to do their jobs.

The other side of the dilemma, though, is that we need adequate and accurate information to manage effectively. As W Charles Redding, a longtime professor of organizational communication at Purdue University wrote, "The higher one goes in the hierarchy, the more must decisions be based upon less and less detailed information of the 'life-facts.' "[1]

Most managers want and need information from employees. Communication that flows from employees to managers for such purposes as asking questions, providing feedback, and making suggestions is called *upward communication.*

Dana Corporation in Toledo, Ohio, once ran a double-page ad titled "Talk Back to the Boss" in an issue of *Newsweek*. The ad stated that productivity at Dana had more than doubled in seven years because Dana recognizes that workers know more about their jobs than bosses and, at Dana, bosses listen to workers.

We need to act to ensure adequate and accurate upward communication—even in the smallest of businesses.

EXAMPLE

I believe that many managers really do believe that if employees have something to say, they should be able to seek managers out and tell them. These are the same managers who brag of an open-door policy for employees and who complain that employees just don't come in. Many of us may have forgotten how great a barrier status in a business can be.

Keith Davis wrote about that barrier this way:

> A manager often does not realize how great the upward communication barriers can be, especially for blue-collar workers. His status and prestige at the plant are different from the workers'. He probably talks differently and dresses differently. He can freely call a worker to his desk or walk to his work station, but the worker is not equally free to call in his manager. The worker usually lacks ability to express himself as clearly as the manager, who is better trained and has more practice in communication skills . . . The worker is further impeded, because he is talking to a person with whose work and responsibilities he is not familiar. The result is that very little upward communication occurs unless management positively encourages it.[2]

Upward communication can be perceived as a risk, and some employees don't want to take that risk.

An Opinion Research Corporation survey of 2,147 employees in eight companies showed that over half agreed with the statement: An employee who told his immediate supervisor everything he felt about the company would probably get into a lot of trouble.

There are so many barriers to adequate and accurate upward communication that a manager *cannot* assume that no news is good news.

Even if employees feel free to express themselves to managers, upward communication presents some special distortion problems.

Employees tend to distort upward communication in a manner that pleases their mangers. Employees tend to tell their managers what they want them to hear and what they want them to know. As a result, good news travels faster upward in an organization than does bad news. Employees are much more likely to communicate messages that make them look good. For example, We exceeded our goals.

Unfortunately, as managers, we also need to know the bad news. For example, We didn't get the orders out on time. Employees tend to tell their managers information that reflects favorably or does not reflect negatively on themselves.

Researchers also report that the more ambitious employees are *less* likely to communicate *anything* to their managers. Ambitious employees are likely to withhold information about job problems from their managers, particularly when the managers' motives and intentions are suspect and their perceived ability to influence an employee's advancement is great.

But even with the built-in barriers and human distortion, managers can act to ensure they get the information they need.

SUGGESTIONS

You may be tempted to ask if encouraging upward communication is worth the effort.

Four reasons why management should value upward communication have been described by Earl Planty and William Machaver both formerly with Johnson & Johnson:[3]

1. It is through upward communication that we learn about our employees so that we can know better how to communicate with them.

2. Upward communication facilitates the acceptance of decisions by encouraging employee participation in the decision-making process, even if it is only discussing the merits and defects of proposed actions.

3. It is through upward communication—what employees say—that we learn whether or not our attempts at communicating with employees have been understood.

4. Regular upward communication encourages the submission of valuable ideas and suggestions.

Therefore, upward communication is indispensable for effective planning and motivation as well as being a source of decision-making information.

Don't be afraid to encourage upward communication—you won't be overwhelmed. Most employees have more of a need to receive information than to send it. The point is for employees to perceive a genuine desire and availability on management's part to listen.

There are many ways to encourage upward communication:

1. *Open-door policies.* Let's admit it. An open-door policy can be a real pain and take a lot of time. But it can be of great, continuing value.

2. *Suggestion systems and letters to management.* Any suggestion system should require that suggestions be signed and that management respond to each suggestion.

When Admiral Zumwalt was in command of the US Navy he printed letters he had received from enlisted personnel and officers in a regular column in a Navy newspaper along with his answers.

3. *Opinion surveys.* Many companies conduct periodic questionnaire surveys.

4. *Meetings.* Patrick Foley, president of Hyatt Hotels, regularly meets with 13 to 16 employees from each hotel in a group for up to three hours to discuss their complaints. Foley looks into every complaint and writes a letter to each person afterward explaining his position.

5. *Informal conversation.* Keith Davis believes the most effective method for encouraging upward communication is sympathetic listening during the many day-to-day informal contacts that occur on the job.

Studies have shown that the accuracy of upward communication is greatest under conditions of high trust. *Trust* in one's superior is the most important factor of open, upward-directed communication.

Finally, it is critical that employees receive responses back. Many suggestion systems, for example, fail because employees perceive no follow-up actions from their suggestions. The response can be No, we can't do this, but *there must be a response* for upward communication to continue.

FOR MORE INFORMATION

For this topic, I think the classic works are still the best:

Davis K. *Human Behavior at Work.* New York, NY: McGraw-Hill Book Company, 1972.

Planty, E, and W Machaver. "Upward Communications: A Project in Executive Development." *Personnel,* January 1952, Vol. 28: pp. 304–18.

Redding, W C. "Position Paper: A Response to Discussions at the Ad Hoc Conference on Organizational Communication." (Paper presented at a meeting of the Ad Hoc Conference on Organizational Communication, University of Missouri at Kansas City, February 1967), quoted in Goldhaber, G M. *Organizational Communication.* 4th ed. Dubuque, IA: William C Brown Publishers, 1986, p. 25.

5. Praising Employees

Problem:

How should I let my employees know they're doing a good job?

Answers:

Relate praise and reprimands to goals and performance standards.

Be very careful with the use of reprimands.

Use immediate and specific praise for work done well.

BACKGROUND

The One Minute Manager was twelve months on the *New York Times Book Review* best seller list. Two years later it was in its twenty-third printing! What is this new management secret?

Written in the style of a children's story by educator and management consultant Kenneth Blanchard and the author of *Value Tales*, Dr. Spencer Johnson, the book has been praised by the likes of Merv Griffin, Earl Nightingale, and *Working Woman* magazine.

Although Blanchard and Johnson may not present us with any new management secrets, they do remind us of three essential management responsibilities.[1]

EXAMPLES

One-Minute Goals

The authors advise employers to make employee responsibilities and accountability clear and, furthermore, to record three to six major goals and performance standards for each employee in 250-word, one-page statements that can be read in less than a minute.

Blanchard and Johnson recommend that both manager and employee periodically review each goal. They also encourage the employee to review his own goals and performance and to see if performance matches goals.

The motivating effect of clearly stated, regularly monitored goals is well recognized. Such goals provide a sense of satisfaction and achievement for the individual and result in an attractive payoff for the company.

One-Minute Praisings

In 1751, Samuel Johnson wrote, "Praise like gold and diamonds owes its value only to its scarcity." Praise, like gold and diamonds, has kept its value and still is a good investment.

Blanchard and Johnson urge managers to tell employees that they plan to tell them how they're doing. And they recommend telling the employees frequently—not just at an annual review. When you catch somebody doing something right, praise that employee immediately!

As a first step, they recommend the employers make physical contact with the employee, such as shaking hands or placing your hand on her shoulder, if that's comfortable for both of you.

Then, look the employee straight in the eye and explain precisely what she did right. Tell the employee how that makes you feel. Encourage her to do more of the same. The whole conversation should last less than a minute.

Small rewards are frequently more effective than large ones.

In essence, it's important to remember to praise employees for good performance. Don't wait for perfect performance! A job done better today than yesterday deserves a one-minute praise.

One-Minute Reprimands

As a manager myself, I have always had difficulty with reprimands. I hire employees, I train them, and I provide them with the tools to do the job. If they don't perform as expected, isn't it my fault in some way? Surely, I feel, employees know they are not performing as expected, so they will soon do something about it. All too frequently, I say nothing for too long—and only I fret about employees' performance.

On the surface, I now believe that Blanchard and Johnson are correct to urge managers to deliver prompt reprimands: immediately upon learning of a mistake, first confirm the facts with the employee. Look the employee directly in the eye and tell him precisely what is wrong.

Then, Blanchard and Johnson urge managers to explain how they feel—such as, angry, annoyed, frustrated. Finally, they urge managers to touch employees and to state how competent they think employees usually are. Be sure that employees understand that you still respect and value them. Again, the whole conversation should last less than a minute.

SUGGESTIONS

Do one-minute praisings and reprimands really improve an employee's performance? To answer that question, we can observe how groups communicate to solve problems. When a group member puts forth an idea that meets with negative responses, that idea usually dies. In a similar fashion, a one-minute reprimand may put an undesired employee behavior to rest.

When a group member puts forth an idea that meets with positive responses, that idea may appear as part of the group's final decision. So again, a one-minute praising may encourage a desired employee behavior to continue.

But what about those ideas that meet with ambiguous reactions—those not clearly positive or negative? Early in a group discussion, ambiguous reactions are interpreted as positive responses, later as negative responses.

Similarly, new employees might interpret a lack of reaction on our part as positive: He hasn't said anything, so everything must be all right. Long-term employees may put a different interpretation on our silence: She must be upset;

she's been so quiet. The problem is employees don't know when we're upset.

In *The One-Minute Manager* children's fairy tale, the authors tell us that being a manager is not as complicated as we think and that managing doesn't take that much time. To this I would add, "and they lived happily ever after."

Blanchard and Johnson borrowed from the behavioral psychologist B F Skinner. Let's go back to the behavioral psychologists for a full picture.

1. Negative reinforcement does produce behavioral change—but often in strange, unpredictable, and undesirable ways. For example, if an employee is reprimanded for being discourteous to a client on the telephone, the employee may associate your reprimand with all client contacts and therefore attempt to avoid them.

2. Positive reinforcement not only shapes behavior but also teaches and, in the process, enhances self-image. For example, if you tell an employee that client X called to compliment the staff on Case No. 12345, you now have an employee who has learned that a specific behavior leads to rewards. And at the same time, the employee creates an enhanced self-image from that success.

[W]e will be more successful in changing behavior with praise than with blame.

Psychologists tell us that we will be more successful in changing behavior with praise than with blame. As Samuel Johnson wrote 200 years ago, praise is dear. Most managers, though, know very little about the effective use of positive reinforcement. These guidelines will help:

1. *Praise must be specific.* Exactly what did the employee do that was praiseworthy?

2. *Praise must be achievable.* No one makes an industry breakthrough everyday, but most of us deserve praise more frequently than at annual reviews.

3. *Praise must be immediate.* On-the-spot bonuses are an example. IBM's Thomas Watson, Sr, used to write bonus checks on the spot for achievements he saw.

In the early days at Foxboro, a scientist presented the president of the company with a much-needed working prototype. Wanting to reward the scientist for a job well done, the president rummaged through his desk to find—a banana! From then on, the highest accolade for scientific achievement at Foxboro has been the "gold banana" pin.

Small rewards are frequently more effective than large ones. The small symbolic praise can become a cause for celebration among friends, while a big bonus can become the focus of a negative political battle.

4. *Praise can be intangible.* For example, the ever-so-meaningful attention from management.

5. *Unpredictable and intermittent praise work better.* Regular praise loses impact, because it comes to be expected.

If the use of praise smacks of visions of the brave new world or arbitrary back patting, you are not alone. Don't we all really want self-motivated employees?

In 1818, John Keats wrote in a letter, "Praise or blame has not but a momentary effect on the man whose love of beauty in the abstract makes him a severe critic of his own works."

What is the source of intrinsic motivation? In many businesses, that source is the practice of having employees establish and work toward production and performance goals they have established themselves. The important element is employee participation in reaching the goal. Pride and commitment are the results.

Effective, productive management takes time—certainly more than just a minute—to involve employees in goal-directed behaviors.

FOR MORE INFORMATION

You'll enjoy any of Ken Blanchard's books. The original in what is now a series was:

Blanchard, K H and Johnson, S. *The One Minute Manager.* New York, NY: Morrow, 1982.

6. Writing Memos and Instructions

Problem:

How can I write more effective memos and instructions?

Answers:

First decide who the reader is and the purpose and subject.

Jot down ideas and then organize them from the reader's perspective.

Edit your writing for simple words and short sentences.

BACKGROUND

Suppose this memorandum just crossed your desk: It is believed that with the parameters that have been imposed by your management, the available marketing program may be hard to evolve. If our program is to impact the consumer to the optimum, meaningful interface with your management may be necessitated.

Your first thought is likely to be, I'd better find a firm that can write English. This mumbo jumbo will never change management's minds. Next, you'd probably start looking for a company that would write the memo like this: "We believe the limits your management has set may prevent the success of our marketing program. To reach our goal, we'll have to ask management to hear our case."

Good business writing is "clear, concise, and natural," says Carol Bradford, a San Francisco-based consultant who teaches a business writing seminar. Writing clearly, concisely, and naturally doesn't come easily to most of us. At one time or another, we've all had trouble finding just the right words when we've had to write an important memo or letter. But, with a little effort, we can overcome many of the barriers to effective business communication.

EXAMPLES

Your writing should be clear and should sound natural. Does it? Take this test using a sample of your business writing and see how readable it is:

1. Select a passage from the text of 100 words or more. Count to the end of the last complete sentence after the 100-word limit. (I've done this for a sample article by counting off the first 113 words under one of the headings.)

2. Count the number of sentences in the sample. (In mine, it's seven.)

3. Divide the number of words by the number of sentences to get the average sentence length. (In mine, it's 113 words divided by 7 sentences = 16.2.)

4. Count the number of words containing three or more syllables. Don't count proper names, combination words such as horsepower or the *ed* or *ing* endings on verbs. (In mine, the total is nine.)

5. Divide this number by the total number of words and multiply by 100 to get a percentage. (In mine, it's [9 divided by 113] × 100 = 7.9 percent.)

6. Add the average sentence length (step 3) and the percentage (step 5) and multiply the result by 0.4. (In mine, its [16.2 + 7.9] × 0.4 = 9.6.)

The result is called your readability level. For comparison, any result between 9 and 12 falls within what's called the easy reading range. *Reader's Digest* averages 10; *Time*, *Newsweek*, and the *Wall Street Journal* average 11. No popular magazine or newspaper exceeds 12.

If your readability level is greater than 12, you're either using sentences that are too long or words that are too complex for clear, concise, natural business writing. Keep most sentences in the active voice of subject, verb, and object—who did what to whom. And keep words simple. English has plenty of monosyllabic words to choose from; Bradford says three-fourths of our words have only one syllable.

Although there is nothing wrong with complex, expressive words, some writers tend to use too many of them. As a result, the meaning of sentences can be muddled and the intent of the correspondence unclear.

The *Guiness Book of World Records* record for the longest sentence is from *The History of the Church of God*. This sentence has more than 3,000 words, 300 commas, and 60 semicolons. To get your point across, keep your writing simple.

SUGGESTIONS

Memos

Before we begin to write a business letter or memo, we decide on its intended reader, its purpose, and its subject.

Good writing is directed to a specific audience. So start by thinking about who will read your message. You'll want to know their backgrounds and experiences and their needs and interests. Consultant Bradford says that, by answering these questions first, you'll become reader-oriented before you write the first word. This is important, because to sell your ideas to your readers you have to communicate in a way that's clear and comfortable to them.

Now that you know who will read your memo or letter, decide what you want to say. Before writing, jot down the points that have to be made. Then organize them, keeping in mind what is most important to the reader. Bradford says that the following techniques increase the effectiveness of any business letter or memo:

1. Provide a title or an *in re* line that summarizes the letter or memo. Choose words that will be familiar to your reader. And be specific. For example, "Revision of delivery schedule" is more accurate than "Changes at ABC Labs."

2. In the first paragraph, state your purpose. Tell the reader why the letter or memorandum is important. A statement such as: "This is to inform you that ABC Labs will ship cases daily via UPS, effective January 1." clearly establishes the purpose of the memo.

3. State conclusions or recommendations early in the memo or letter. Writing specialist Rudolph Flesch calls this spilling your beans up front. Don't expect your readers to search through your writing to find out what you want them to do. For example, the following sentences get to the point quickly: "Please note: If you would like different shipping

arrangements, you must specify so on your order. Changes made after we've received your order will be subject to a service charge."

Before writing, jot down the points that have to be made. Then organize them, keeping in mind what is most important to the reader.

4. Organize your ideas, from the most important to the least important from the reader's point of view.

If you've ever tried to follow the directions to assemble a child's toy on a birthday morning or to find the trunk latch on a new automobile with the help of the owner's manual, you know that writing clear, effective instructions is a skill.

Instructions

Instructions tell the reader how to do something or how to make something. Almost everyone with a responsible job writes instructions—from how to use equipment to what needs to be done during vacation.

The general rule to keep in mind is that instructions should emphasize the reader's role, explaining each step in enough detail so the readers can complete the procedure safely and efficiently. You can use the following guidelines:

1. *Address the appropriate technical level.* Give consideration to your audience. It is easy to assume that others know more than they do, especially about a task you now do almost automatically. If you are not sure if the readers have any technical background or technical skills, write for the general reader.

Assume that if your readers are professional colleagues, they know a little less than you do; a general reader will know a great deal less or nothing at all.

2. *Provide some background information.* Before you can describe how, you need to explain what and why. It's a good practice to begin with the reason for the instructions, then

to state your assumptions about the reader's level of technical understanding, and finally to define any special terms before even beginning the step-by-step instructions.

3. *Logically order the steps.* Good instructions not only divide a process into steps, they must also guide readers through the steps in order. Explain the steps in chronological order as they are to be performed.

4. *Use visual aids.* Whenever possible, use a picture, a diagram, or a drawing to illustrate a step.

5. *Place warnings and cautions strategically.* The only things that should interrupt the step-by-step procedure are warnings and cautions. Warnings and cautions should be clearly set out immediately before the step to which they apply.

6. *Live up to the title.* Make the title say exactly what your instructions will deliver, no more and no less.

Of all writing, instructions require the most clarity. Readers want to be able to perform the action—at least in their minds—as they read your directions. Readers don't want to have to read all the directions first, let alone study them, before beginning. Four writing tips result in clear directions:

1. *Always use active verbs.* For example, use *turn the valve*, rather than *the valve should be turned.* Active verb phrases are more visual and direct.

2. *Use transitional words to lead the reader through the steps.* Use words such as *first, next,* and *after.*

3. *Make the phrasing of the steps parallel. Always use, use,* and *make* (in tips 1 through 3) are parallel. *Always use, using,* and *how to make* are not parallel. Parallel phrasing is more readable.

4. *Use short sentences and short paragraphs.* Edit out unnecessary information.

Writing descriptions of how to do something and explaining how something works are almost identical to writing instructions for someone else. Each process can be broken down into individual steps.

FOR MORE INFORMATION

There are several good references in the business section of your local bookstore. Here's one:

Reimold, C. *How to Write a Million Dollar Memo.* New York, NY: Dell, 1984.

7. Turning Conflicts into Agreements

Problem:

How can I apply my negotiation skills to different types of conflict issues?

Answers:

Determine your objective, demand, and fallback position.

Determine the other party's objective.

Use negotiation skills to make it possible for each of you to reach your objectives.

BACKGROUND

While negotiation may be most often thought of as the means of dealing with labor-management contract disputes, negotiation skills can be applied to the full spectrum of human conflicts.

Negotiation as a means of conflict resolution should be limited to situations in which the disputing parties are perceived to have relatively equal power. Without that perception, the party with greater power can simply impose a solution. Often the first step of effective conflict resolution through negotiation is the establishment of the perception of relatively equal power between the parties.

Additionally negotiators must accept that each person sees the conflict differently and, by extension then, the concept of right and wrong is not a useful approach. A disputant will perceive himself as right. That implies that the other disputant is wrong and that the strategy can become one of persuading the party in the wrong to change position. Simply putting aside the right and wrong concept can facilitate moving into a negotiating and problem-solving mode.

Finally, the overall goals for negotiation must be considered. Most commonly, these are stated as win-lose or win-win. The so-called hardball negotiating techniques are most often associated with win-lose negotiation in which one party's objectives are achieved at the expense of the opposing party. Win-win negotiating, on the other hand, results in an outcome that achieves the goals of both parties. In win-win negotiating, then, maintaining a working relationship is as important as the outcome itself.

It is a misconception to think of win-win negotiating as a softer form of negotiating resulting in compromises. In fact, in win-win negotiating one works hard to make it possible for the opposing party to achieve their objective. Win-win negotiating calls for more creativity and communication and encourages a harmonious, long-term relationship.

EXAMPLES

To illustrate negotiation principles, it is useful to look at different kinds of negotiation based on how the issues differ.

Single-Issue Numerical Conflicts

Negotiations involving only one quantitative issue, such as money, can be called single-issue numerical negotiation. Usually, single-issue numerical conflicts are resolved by compromise.

Because of the use of compromise as the most typical resolution technique, single-issue numerical conflicts best illustrate the concept of positional bargaining. Effective positional bargaining requires the setting of three "positions" before the negotiations begin:

1. *Best Alternative to a Negotiated Agreement (BATANA).* Before any negotiation, one must evaluate the consequences of not settling. One must know before the negotiation begins what will happen if no agreement is reached. If one determines the consequences are disastrous, one should attempt to put a more favorable alternative into place before the negotiation begins.

2. *Objective.* A commonly made mistake in negotiation is the failure to determine one's objective before the negotiation. This mistake can be heard in comments such as, Get the best deal you can. Without a predetermined objective during the negotiation, one is more likely to be swayed as to what is reasonable by the opponent's arguments. A predetermined objective gives one a goal. Of course, that goal can be modified as appropriate during the negotiation.

Traditionally, an objective was called the *mini* or *minimum* to represent the minimum one would accept. The minimum, or objective, should be treated as private information.

3. *Demand.* Since single-issue numerical negotiation is resolved by compromise, logically one must set her public

demand position far enough out to be able to compromise back to her objective. Another common mistake is to make one's objective equal to one's demand. When this is done, negotiations are difficult to resolve, because any compromise will result in a losing outcome.

But what motivates negotiators to settle? What motivates negotiators to start compromising? In single-issue numerical negotiation and in most other negotiations, the strongest motivation to settle is the *deadline.* Deadline pressure forces negotiators to compromise or settle for their BATANA.

Most settlements are reached as a function of the deadline. Moving the deadline back only delays the settlement. When there is ample time, the communication tends to be about demands, justifications, and persuasion. As the deadline approaches, the communication becomes focused on specific proposals for compromise.

The most compelling deadlines are objective ones, such as the expiration of a contract, a date in court, or the start or end of well-established budget cycles, based on an independent phenomenon that affects both negotiators.

What happens, though, if the demand a party sets is clearly unreasonable? With the strength of the BATANA in mind, say you find the offer unreasonable but you remain willing to negotiate when presented a reasonable offer.

Single-Issue Nonnumerical Conflicts

Of course, many negotiations over a single issue are not numerical. In fact, many of our most difficult conflicts—the escalated conflicts—are over nonnumerical single issues. An example includes employee performance appraisals in which the question is, Was the standard met or not?

Single-issue nonnumerical conflicts are difficult to resolve for many reasons: The parties see themselves on opposite sides. They are often yes-no issues. The probability of winning appears remote. Each concession by one party must be met with an equal concession by the other party. But the nonnumerical issues don't admit themselves to partial concessions.

The critical skill, then, for resolving single-issue nonnumerical conflicts is to *unpack* the single issue into multiple issues. To unpack a single issue, determine all the components of the disagreement. This changes the single-issue conflict into multiple-issue conflict. Then the conflict can be negotiated using multiple-issue skills.

Multiple-Issue Conflict

Let's begin by comparing single issue to multiple issue:

First, multiple-issue positional negotiation still involves the setting of the same three positions: the BATANA, the objective, and the demand. The only difference is that these positions are established on multiple issues.

Second, multiple-issue positional negotiation can be motivated to settlement by the deadline. Deadline awareness is still critical as a form of motivation to settle.

Now, let's look at the differences: Remember, single issue negotiation is almost always settled through compromise. And because of that, the only position we need to work with is the demands, since the compromise is based on the demands. In multiple-issue negotiation, it is critical to have information about the other party's objective.

Remember, our objective is to establish a win-win outcome, an outcome that meets each party's objective. To do that requires some idea of what the other party wants. And it requires giving the other party some idea of what you need in the settlement. We can only begin to construct a win-win outcome when we have information about the other party's objective.

SUGGESTIONS

How does one determine the other party's objective? There are several skills. Among the most important are listening, asking open-ended and probe questions, mirroring back tentative understanding, and asking "what-if" questions.

Listening

Negotiation is a skill of listening—not of talking. If our objective is a win-win outcome, the only way that is possible is by knowing the other party's objective. That requires listening.

Asking Open-Ended and Probe Questions

Listening requires that the other party talk. To achieve that, the effective negotiator asks open-ended questions that permit long, unstructured responses. In this response, we're listening for clues as to what is important for the party. Use probe questions to ask for additional information.

Mirroring Back Tentative Understanding

By carefully paraphrasing what we have heard, we assure the other party that we understand their points.

Asking "What-if" Questions

The what-if questions are critical to negotiation. These hypothetical and conditional questions test our understanding of what we have heard of the other party's objective. An effective what-if question must be worded to be clearly understood as a proposal for discussion, not as an offer.

At the same time you are securing information about your opponent's objectives, you need to be giving information to the opponent about your objective. I have often been asked if it is more difficult to negotiate with professionals or amateurs. You should see that the answer is clearly amateurs, because they frequently withhold all the information about their objectives.

Knowing your objective and being prepared with some information about your opponent's objective, you can proceed with multiple-issue negotiation. But it proceeds differently than the simple compromise so typical of single-issue numerical negotiation. The more common procedure is to link movement on one issue in exchange for movement on another issue. This eliminates the problem of equivalency of concessions. Movement on one issue is equal to movement on another issue, because the parties agree to it. The equivalency is otherwise not obvious. It is the linking of issues that is characteristic of multiple-issue negotiation.

The critical steps in preparation for negotiation include development of BATANA, demand, and objective positions. The facts to back up the demands should be identified.

Equal attention should be given to identifying the needs of the other party, verifying facts they might present, and developing options that might lead to win-win outcomes.

FOR MORE INFORMATION

Of course, I'm going to recommend my own book here:

Jandt, F E. *Win-Win Negotiating: Turning Conflict Into Agreement.* New York, NY: Wiley, 1985.

8. Giving a Speech

Problem:

I have to give a talk! How do I make a speech?

Answers:

Develop a clear idea of your purpose and audience.
Prepare outline, introduction, and conclusion.
Develop visual aids.

BACKGROUND

When most of us think of giving a speech, we think of formal settings. And, most of us (60 to 70 percent according to my surveys) have significant symptoms of stage fright. These symptoms can include sweaty palms, throat and body tension, and vocal hesitations—the ahms and ahs.

A study reported in the *Chicago Tribune* found that beyond a person's entry-level job, specialized college training was less important for success than general skills in interpersonal relations, oral and written communication, and general business know-how. Another study reported in the *Chicago Tribune* found that speaking clearly and forcefully with others is important in almost all positions held by college graduates and, moreover, that it is crucial for administrators, managers, sales personnel, allied health workers, educators, social workers, and counselors.

Actually, most of our public speaking is in informal settings. The basics were developed some 2,500 years ago and haven't changed that much.

EXAMPLES

Most of us fear public speaking because of a fear of failing. I tell speakers that this kind of fear is a natural biological process that can energize us to take on an important challenge. I am more concerned about speakers who don't experience stage fright. To me, it means they're not challenged by the situation to do their best.

Biologically, our pulse rate and perspiration can increase, and we can experience dry mouth, shaking hands and knees, shortness of breath, and a nervous stomach. These can all be controlled. Follow these steps:

- Be thoroughly prepared; that is, follow the preparation steps described later—and then rehearse.
- Visualize and expect positive results from your speech.
- Recognize any fear as a natural response of an energized person.
- Use physical control, such as taking a step or two, gesturing with your hand, or tightening the muscles in your arms and legs, to use up excess energy.

SUGGESTIONS

For 20 years, I've taught people how to speak publicly with greater self-confidence and improved results. These steps will help you in any public speaking situation.

As with writing memos and letters, the first step is to have a clear idea of your purpose or desired outcome, exactly what you want the main point of your speech to be, and who your audience is.

When thinking about your purpose, project how you want your audience to respond. Think of your main point as a one-sentence summary of your entire speech. Many unsuccessful speeches ramble on, because speakers don't know what their main point is. Successful speakers preplan their main point and then develop their speech from that.

All speeches should be audience-directed. Analyze the audience before you begin to develop a speech beyond the main point. Answer these questions about your audience:

- What do they already know about your topic?
- Are they already interested in your topic?
- What is their attitude toward your topic? Do they agree or disagree?

- What do you know about the demographic characteristics of the audience? For instance, is it all men or all women; are they high schoolers or retired?
- What do you know about the audience's interests? What will the audience be expecting to hear?

Use the answers to these questions to guide you as you think about just how to develop your main point.

The second step is to outline your thoughts. How do you write a successful speech? The answer to this is easy—you don't. The word *speech* means spoken words. If you or I write a speech, we write an essay and then read it aloud. Unfortunately, it is very difficult to write an essay the way people actually speak. That's why professional speech writers are paid so much. Audiences expect to hear a speaker speaking naturally. You and I probably cannot write a speech.

A method that works for most people is to prepare an outline and then rehearse the speech from abbreviated notes based on that outline. Outlining is simple. It doesn't need to be a school exercise:

1. Take your main point and write out three to five points that develop or explain that main point. Try to limit the main points to a maximum of five—that's about all an audience can remember from *listening* alone.

2. Put those main points in some logical order. The most typical ways are to order them by time (what was or should be done first, second, etc.), by space or geography, by problem followed by solution, or by the advantages followed by disadvantages. The idea is to put these three to five points in some logical, easily followed sequence.

3. Go to each point in turn and write out subpoints of explanation, amplification, example, illustration, and statistics or quotations.

4. Go back to each subpoint in turn and write out sub-subpoints if necessary.

The most effective subpoints are those that encourage the audience to think visually.

Preparing speeches in this fashion forces us to stay on one main point and then develop it in an organized way.

In my experience, the most effective subpoints are those that encourage the audience to think visually. Audiences listen to and remember the stories, illustrations, and examples.

To finish up, plan an introduction, conclusion, and sign posts to help the listener.

The introduction should lead the audience to form a favorable first impression of you and begin focusing on your main point. This can be accomplished with humor, anecdotes, quotations, startling statistics, rhetorical questions and references to the audience, occasion, or subject.

The conclusion should refocus the audience's thinking on your main idea. Most good conclusions provide a brief summary and link back to the introduction in some way. The conclusion should be short. When you're finished, sit down. Don't go on and on for five minutes, repeating what you've already said.

Finally, remember to use sign posts. A speech is immediate; a listener can't go back to a point missed. Speakers need to help listeners follow the speech with sign posts. Some examples are:

- "I have three points to make today. First, let me turn to . . ."
- "Now that we've seen why . . . let's look at . . ."
- "The last of my three reasons is . . ."

Robert Craig, chief of the U.S. Public Health Service Audio Visual Facility, reported some startling research. When people are taught by words alone, their immediate recall of the material is 70 percent. Three days later it is 10 percent. But when people are told *and shown*, immediate recall is 85 percent. Three days later it is still 65 percent complete!

Whenever possible, think of ways to visually illustrate your speech with objects and demonstrations, charts and diagrams, and handouts and pictures.

Becoming a competent public speaker is not difficult, but it does require discarding some ideas of what a speech is, and it requires thorough preparation.

FOR MORE INFORMATION

There are several good references in the business section of your local bookstore. Here's one:

Richards, I. *How to Give a Successful Presentation.* London: Graham & Tretman, 1988.

II

PERSONAL EFFECTIVENESS

9. Time Management

Problem:

How can I gain control of my time?

Answers:

Record how you use your time now.
Compare how you use time now to your objectives.
Use your objectives to schedule your time.

BACKGROUND

It wasn't until the late 1970s that the term *time management* came into common use. By the early 1980s, managers were thinking of time as a resource to be managed.

Much of the credit for this trend should go to R Alec MacKenzie, a management consultant and author of the American Management Association book *The Time Trap.*[1] His book and an interview he did for *U.S. News & World Report*[2] are still the leaders in helping managers control how they use their time.

EXAMPLE

Suppose an employee wastes an hour a day on the job. What does that loss mean, in dollars and cents, to an employer? Assuming the employee works eight hours a day and has three weeks of vacation and nine holidays annually, here are the costs of a wasted hour per day over the course of a year at various salary levels:

Salary	Cost to Employer
$ 20,000	$ 2,500
25,000	3,125
30,000	3,750
35,000	4,375
40,000	5,000
50,000	6,250
75,000	9,375
100,000	12,500

Based on his experience with managers, MacKenzie ranks the 15 major time wasters as:

1. Telephone interruptions.
2. Visitors dropping in without appointments.

3. Meetings, both scheduled and unscheduled.
4. Crisis situations for which no plans were possible.
5. Lack of objectives, priorities, and deadlines.
6. Cluttered desk and personal disorganization.
7. Involvement in routine and detail that should be delegated to others.
8. Attempting too much at once and underestimating the time it takes to do it.
9. Failure to set up clear lines of responsibility and authority.
10. Inadequate, inaccurate, or delayed information from others.
11. Indecision and procrastination.
12. Unclear or lack of communication and instruction.
13. Inability to say no.
14. Lack of standards and progress reports that enable a company manager to keep track of developments.
15. Fatigue.

SUGGESTIONS

The Telephone

The telephone is a great time-saving instrument, but for many managers it can become the biggest time waster. Some managers answer their own phones. Others talk with every caller. Still others fail to deal with the caller fully, forcing the caller to call again and again.

MacKenzie recommends that a qualified, professional secretary take all calls. A good secretary should be able to completely handle at least half of all calls, divert others to the people most qualified to handle them, and prepare information for the remaining few you should return yourself.

No secretary? Use an answering machine or service, so you can have uninterrupted work time.

Once you're on the telephone, remember to limit your time. Prepare polite and clever ways to explain to callers that you're busy and need to get to the point.

Drop-In Visitors

MacKenzie believes that an open-door policy destroys a manager's effectiveness faster than any other business policy. Closing the door for periods of undisturbed concentration is most effective.

When a co-worker drops in and says, "Have you got a minute? our answer too frequently is, "Sure, what's on your mind?" Effective time-management responses, on the other hand, include, "It all depends. What is it?" "I'm in the middle of something now. Can we get together over lunch or later in the day?" "We're going to have our regular meeting tomorrow. Can it wait until then?"

I've found it effective to remove all visitor's chairs from my office. Visitors are much more time efficient when they have to stand. If it's important, we can quickly get a chair.

Meetings

Nine out of 10 businesspeople say one-half of the time they spend in meetings is wasted. If managers spend 10 hours a week in meetings, then 5 hours a week is wasted, reducing their effectiveness by 12½ percent.

Remember, no other activity can expand to fill the time as easily as a meeting. MacKenzie recommends various techniques for controlling meeting time:

- Start and end on time.
- Have a "time remaining" clock visible to show how many minutes are left.

- Keep to the agenda.
- Invite only those whose attendance is really needed.
- Resist interruptions.
- Summarize and distribute the results in writing with follow-up assignments.
- Use stand-up meetings whenever possible.

Delegation

MacKenzie recommends immediate decisions be made about 80 percent of the items that come to your desk. You won't know any better about them tomorrow or the day after. The basic message is move the work off your desk. Don't let it stack up.

Second, delegate as much work as you can to others. If you don't delegate, you'll get buried and little will get done. General Dwight D. Eisenhower had a policy that nothing was permitted to be brought to him unless it was both urgent and important. If it wasn't urgent, it could wait. If it wasn't important, somebody else could handle it.

You don't need to put in long hours to be successful. In fact, Clarence Randall, former chairman of Inland Steel, referred to this as the myth of the overworked executive. People are overworked because they want to be. The long hours some people put in frequently result in making them less effective, because their judgment becomes impaired and their motivation destroyed.

The first step in gaining control of your time is to determine how you use your time now. Time is a unique resource; everyone has the same amount of it every day. Time is not the problem; it's how we use it.

Keep a log for a week of how you use your time. Every fifteen minutes jot down what you're doing. At the end of a week review your time log and see where your time is going. Successful professionals always have before them the objectives they want to accomplish on both a long-range and short-range basis. Relate how you use your time to your objectives. Are you really devoting time to your objectives? Anything that prevents you from achieving those objectives is a time waster.

Most time management manuals tell you to order each day's planned activities the first thing each morning:

A priorities *advance* your objectives. These should produce the maximum results for you over time.

B priorities *back up* your *A* priorities. These should be the day-to-day, week-to-week maintenance tasks necessary for stability in an ongoing operation. Such things as returning phone calls and record keeping are *B* priorities.

C priorities are the *can-dos* if you have the time. These should be the short-time tasks that are not absolutely necessary. Reorganizing the files and having lunch with a casual acquaintance are *C* priorities.

Put your *A*s in one, two, three order, and put your *B*s in one, two, three order. Then start your day on *A-1*. When that is finished, go on to *A-2*.

Remember, time management is really self-discipline. Before you can master time, you have to master yourself.

FOR MORE INFORMATION

There are many guides available. I like MacKenzie's:

MacKenzie, R A. *The Time Trap*. New York, NY: Amacom, 1990.

10.   The Organized Desk

Problem:

How can I keep myself organized?

Answers:

Critically evaluate your clutter. Throw out what isn't saving you time or money or improving the quality of your life.

Adopt a system to keep your work area uncluttered.

BACKGROUND

Let's take an instant assessment of your office desk. Check off those that are true for you:

_____ A leaning tower in your "in" box.

_____ Stacks of paper on your desk.

_____ Open files on your desk.

_____ "Someday" files (as in someday I'll get to this) on your desk.

_____ Written reminders on odd-sized scraps of paper strewn about your desk.

_____ Phone message slips scattered about.

_____ Multiple calendars.

Did you check off only a few? Did you check off most of them? Did you check off all of them? If you checked most or all of them, you should have entered the competition for the messiest desk in Washington held by the District of Columbia consulting firm, Priority Management.

I conducted a random survey to see how people with cluttered desks are viewed negatively. The most commonly used descriptive phrases were:

• Unorganized.
• Sloppy, messy, and dirty.
• Looks busy but doesn't get work done.
• Lazy.

Then I asked how they viewed people with clean desks positively:

• Well organized.
• Neat.
• Productive.
• Clean.

EXAMPLES

Being a person who admits to having a cluttered desk on occasion, I also asked, in my random sample, how people with clean desks are viewed negatively. The most commonly used descriptive phrases were:

- Nothing to do, bored, not involved.
- Never works.
- Puts work on others.
- Mean, cold, unfeeling, not friendly, no personality.
- Neat freak, insane, paranoid.
- Perfectionist.

And I also asked how people with cluttered desks were viewed positively:

- Very busy.
- Works hard, involved, good source of information.
- Easy to talk to, personable, approachable.

But to be fair, as a writer and consultant, I often benefit from collecting clutter. It's from the clutter I get my treasure of ideas and examples for articles. If I were in a research staff position, I could make similar use of the clutter. But, as a line manager, the clutter would be trash.

A cluttered desk can hold you at your current level of effectiveness. You're working with and at the same material day in, day out.

If you can't deal with your clutter yourself, there is help available. You can take training courses in time management. Priority Management, for example, will train you to arrange your day, manage your time, keep your files, and learn to prioritize. You can also hire personal consultants—professional, hands-on organizers or "clutter busters" charge as much as $250 an hour. They contend that being organized is not an end in itself. Rather, it is a way of gaining more control over your life.

They also feel that going through old stuff can often trigger emotional memories. Like psychotherapists, they encourage customers to release or complete the unfinished, emotionally charged business that typically hides behind disorder. For example, some assert that adult children of alcoholics, who grew up in chaotic homes, may unconsciously use clutter to recreate the level of chaos they were comfortable with as children.

Are personal consultants worth the money? Lee Larsen, vice president and general manager of radio station KOA in Denver, said, "It was definitely worth it financially. And it continues to be worth it . . . You want that organized, tidy, in-control kind of feeling. We [the radio station] learned, in fact, that we are not the national archive. We used to think we were. We had to save everything just in case somebody in the world might need it."

SUGGESTIONS

If you'd like to have the positive image, then you have to change your work habits. You'll have to set the objective of having only one piece of business on your desk at a time. Everything else must be stored in files. The only possible exception to the one-piece-of-work rule is a pad of paper with a list of things you have to do.

> . . . *being organized is not an end in itself. Rather, it is a way of gaining more control over your life.*

You can get organized yourself. But to do so you have to ask yourself three general questions and then ask yourself four "trash/treasure" questions about each item on your desk.

First, ask yourself the general questions: Who am I? Where am I going? What do I need to get there?

Then, ask yourself the trash/treasure questions: Does this thing make me money? Does this thing save me money? Does this thing save me time? Does this thing improve the quality of my life?

If something on your desk doesn't do one of these things for you, trash it. Don't use closet organizers. They're just another way to store junk. Don't buy another file cabinet. They're just a way to store junk vertically. While the above questions are important, you can't get rid of something just because it hasn't been used for a long time. For example, you don't want to get rid of a fire extinguisher simply because you haven't used it.

After you've cleaned up the clutter, you'll need a system to keep it clean. Professional organizers recommend the "T-R-A-F" method. Each memo, piece of mail, and other paper should immediately be handled in one of four ways:

T—Throw it out.

R—Refer it to someone else.

A—Take action on it.

F—File it.

After you've cleaned up the clutter, you'll need a system to keep it clean.

On the other hand, when you reach the objective of "one piece of work" on your desk at a time, the clutter busters claim you will experience these advantages:

- Have a feeling of serenity and possibility.
- Get home earlier, more time for yourself and your family.
- Have energy to concentrate on new projects.
- Get through projects that were long dormant.
- Make more money with less effort.
- Add velocity to you career progress.

11. Getting a New Idea Adopted

Problem:

How can I get others to go along with new ideas?

Answers:

Compare your innovation to ideas that have been successfully introduced in the past.

Use a systematic, step-by-step plan to introduce change.

BACKGROUND

Creativity and innovation continue to be critical management concerns. Employee creativity is seen as one way for businesses and organizations to be responsive to change. Much of that pressure for internal change results from the external, fast-changing world around us. Change produces problems, and problems require creative solutions.

There are at least two ways for a business or organization to encourage creativity and innovation. One is to take the structural approach by establishing management practices that facilitate new ideas rather than squelch them. Structural approaches range from suggestion systems to incentive awards for innovative ideas to specially designated innovation teams.

The second approach is to teach employees to think more creatively. Perhaps the best approach is to combine the first and second approaches.

Roger Von Oech, author of *A Whack on the Side of the Head*, suggests that to become more creative, we first need to reject eight common beliefs:[1]

1. *Find the right answer.* In school, we are all taught that there is one right answer to every problem. However, there is no one right answer. Most problems are open-ended. The first answer may be obvious, but the second, third, and fourth are creative.

2. *That's not logical.* Hard, logical thinking can be the death of new ideas. Even contradictory alternatives should be considered.

3. *Follow the rules.* To get a creative idea, you often have to break the rules that no longer make sense. Ask: Why have we always done it this way? Should we continue to do it this way? What opportunities does change create?

4. *Be practical.* Ideas need the wide realm of the possible, rather than the narrow one of the practical to grow. Begin by asking, What if . . . ?

5. *Don't be foolish.* When faced with a problem, let yourself play. Risk being foolish. Then write down the ideas that come to you.

6. *Don't make mistakes.* Mistakes can simply be stepping-stones in the creative process.

7. *That's not my area.* Good, fresh ideas almost invariably come from outside our own area. We have to see what ideas are out there that we can use in our area.

8. *I'm not creative.* There is something of a self-fulfilling prophecy here. People who see themselves as creative usually are creative.

EXAMPLES

M O Edwards, president of Idea Development Associates of Palo Alto, California, clearly distinguishes between problem solving and creativity. In problem solving, you start with a well-defined problem to solve. The problem statement includes the essential criteria that a solution must meet.

The problem is tackled with *vertical* thinking, that is, logically. Facts and clinical judgment are central to the process.

Relatively few ideas or alternative solutions are sought or obtained. Ideas or proposed solutions are evaluated by using the criteria established in the problem statement as soon as they are suggested.

Logical problem-solving approaches work best when the identified problem has some cause that can be identified.

The solution accepted must be corrective. That is, it must fix something that was wrong. Thus, action taken can be easily evaluated: Did they fix what was wrong?

The Japanese word for creativity—satori—connotes the understanding that insight and enlightenment are the products of patience and practice.

On the other hand, in creativity, the problem is vague and ill defined. Part of the creative approach is to define, or perceive, the problem in different ways. Problems are viewed as opportunities or challenges rather than as problems to be fixed. Few if any criteria to evaluate solutions are considered early in the process because criteria limit creativity.

The problem is tackled with *lateral* thinking, that is, open-ended, illogical, nonlinear, and intuitive. Facts are considered, but they are not central to the process. Creative thinking should result in what is called the *aha!* experience, an intuitive insight that is not obvious by logic. Creativity does not necessarily come easily. The Japanese word for creativity—*satori*—connotes the understanding that insight and enlightenment are the products of patience and practice.

As many ideas and alternative solutions as possible are generated. Evaluation of ideas is delayed as long as possible.

Creative approaches work best for problems that have no single, definite cause and when you're seeking opportunities rather than fixing things that have gone wrong.

Solutions often involve discovering a new challenge or opportunity that may launch the whole process over again.

Peter Ueberroth credits creative thinking skills with helping him bring in the 1984 Los Angeles Olympics with a $250 million surplus instead of the usual loss.

I believe anyone can be creative if they rid themselves of these beliefs and if they apply themselves to creative problem solving.

Have you ever seen the spectacular TWA building at New York's JFK Airport? It was described by an architectural magazine as ". . . a totality of fluid form curving and circling within itself . . ." suggesting ". . . the flight of a great bird." Actually, architect Eero Saarinen got the idea from the curved shell of half a grapefruit. One morning he carved arches in his grapefruit half and turned it over and there it was—a creative idea for a building!

SUGGESTIONS

Psychologist and management consultant Harvey A Hornstein has published the results of a study of 157 US and 51 Japanese managers.[2] The managers in Hornstein's survey reported succeeding at implementing innovative ideas in their organizations two-thirds of the time. From his study of their experiences, Hornstein developed five guidelines for successfully introducing new ideas:

1. *Watch your focus.* Stick to business issues or frame your concern as a business issue. A focus on the *performance of superiors* was least likely to succeed and most likely to result in a negative response. A focus on *subordinates* had little risk but also little positive reward. Others don't see our focusing on subordinates as anything more than our regular job. A focus on *ethical* matters had a risk of failure and no reward for the organization. It is only a focus on *business* issues that has the least risk of failure and the greatest positive organizational reward. In other words, stick to the knitting!

2. *Watch your credibility.* Generally speaking, credibility is affected by one's image of *expertise.* As a result, the changes you propose in your area of expertise are more likely to succeed. A technician with no recognized background in accounting is not likely to be able to change a business's billing procedures.

3. *Be direct.* Being *indirect* means to use long, drawn-out procedures like memorandums, letters, and reports that keep the parties involved at arm's length. Being *direct* means to act with conviction and determination. In US culture, acting directly is more likely to succeed and more likely to be rewarded.

4. *Create supporters.* Few individuals can create change without supporters. Meet with people who will be affected. Work to make them a part of the team that wants the change.

5. *Propose solutions to problems that have caused pain.* This guideline relates to *timing.* After experiencing some discom-

fort, people are more ready to accept change. We've all heard the saying, Build a better mousetrap and the world will beat a path to your door. Not true if there is no mouse problem.

Hornstein's guidelines can guide your thinking before proposing a change.

For several years, I've been a consultant with the 15,000-employee California Department of Transportation. My job has been to work with their training department to design and teach a management training course for their mid-level managers. I provide them with the skills to influence and change their organization by successfully introducing new ideas. I devised a seven-step plan for them that can be used by anyone planning to institute a change into any organization:

1. *Problem Awareness.* Your first step is to define your proposed change as a *business* problem in your area of *expertise*—one that has caused some *discomfort* for the organization.

2. *Establish Your Objective.* All too often, people have no clear idea of the change they desire. Instead they say, Something has to be done about . . . and they create a lot of confusion, getting people involved in the problem, but offering them no chance to solve the problem. You need both to define the problem and develop a clear understanding for yourself of the change you want.

3. *Identify Interested Parties.* Before you can begin to develop supporters, you need to identify *everyone* who will be affected by this change—both directly and indirectly. I recommend making a comprehensive list of each person or group who will be affected.

4. *Assess Their Needs, Interests, and Values.* After you have developed a list of people affected by the proposed change, go back and identify the needs and interests of each person involved.

For example, if you are proposing a new billing procedure, then business owners, office staff, and customers are directly involved. Owners want good customer relations and prompt payments; office staff might feel comfortable with the existing procedure; customers want to be treated fairly and kept informed of any changes.

5. *Assess Your Resources.* I find that people proposing changes frequently neglect to assess their own resources or the power they have in the situation. Your *expertise* is one resource. Identify the other resources you have to bring about this change.

6. *Identify Possible Compromise Areas.* Here's the hard, creative part. Keeping your objective in mind and recognizing the interests other parties have, develop compromises that make it possible for you to reach your objective while satisfying the interests of the other parties.

For example, for the new billing procedure, you might need to meet with the owners to explain how the change will result in faster payments while still maintaining good will. You might need to meet several times with office staff to discover problems with the existing procedure that the new procedure will correct. Finally, you might want the office staff to help draft a letter explaining the new billing procedure to your customers.

7. *Action (Develop, Implement, and Evaluate Your Strategies).* Don't just drop off a suggestion. Remember to take direct action yourself.

Every change in a business is going to present a problem for someone. Planning to introduce change will make it more likely for the change to be implemented and accepted.

What is top management's role in all of this? Perhaps it's easier to begin with what top management should not do.

Hornstein uses the term *ideacide* to refer to the premature murder of an idea before it is appropriately and adequately explored. You've heard the phrase "Fifty Ways to Leave Your Lover." Hornstein gives us 14 ways to kill an idea:

1. The boss won't like it.
2. It's not policy.
3. I don't have the authority.

4. We're not in the (fill in with the name of any industry other than the organization's) business.
5. Does (fill in with a competitor's name) do it?
6. Too much risk.
7. It's not my job (or your job, or their job).
8. Not invented here (NIH).
9. It's never been tried.
10. We've always done it this way.
11. There's no precedent.
12. It's not in the budget.
13. Why rock the boat?
14. Send it to committee!

All businesses face the dilemma of dealing with employee's ideas for change. On one hand, employees frequently have the direct experience from which new ideas for new ways of doing things can arise.

On the other hand, most employees are dissuaded from questioning established practice, because they believe conformity is rewarded with perks and promotions. Those who don't conform can be fired, given minimal or no salary increase, be passed over for promotion, and excluded from groups.

Organizational realities often stifle employee-generated ideas that can keep a business alive. In order to remain competitive, every business must balance conventional behavior essential to smooth daily functioning and creativity essential to progress, although perhaps inconsistent with existing practices.

FOR MORE INFORMATION

Hornstein, H A. *Managerial Courage: Revitalizing Your Company Without Sacrificing Your Job.* New York, NY: John Wiley & Sons, 1986.

Von Oech, R. *A Whack on the Side of the Head.* New York, NY: Warner Books, 1983.

12. Managing Anger

Problem:

How should I handle anger at work?

Answers:

Learn to express your anger in a productive way.

Allow others to express their anger before you attempt to confront the problem.

BACKGROUND

"People on the job are afraid to deal with their anger. I don't know of any office where it's considered ok to be angry," says Robert Cromey, a licensed family counselor who has conducted management seminars on anger at work before becoming rector of San Francisco's Trinity Episcopal Church.

"Surprisingly, the most prevalent problem I've come across is that managers often feel they can't express anger at their subordinates, while I don't hear of too many problems the other way around," says Cromey.

"We see all the symptoms of anger: absenteeism, low productivity, high employee turnover, sabotage. We also see symptoms of turning inward: drug addiction, alcoholism.

"My position is that anger is normal. It's a matter of how you express it."

EXAMPLES

Anger is a social emotion. It is a reaction when our needs or desires are blocked, particularly if that block seems arbitrary or unreasonable.

For example, when smoking was permitted on the airlines, I saw passengers calmly put out their cigarettes upon hearing the announcement: "For your safety, FAA rules and regulations prohibit smoking during takeoff and landing." It was considered a completely reasonable request.

Anger is a social emotion. It is a reaction when our needs or desires are blocked, particularly if that block seems arbitrary or unreasonable.

I remember seeing one passenger who arrived too late for a seat assignment in the smoking section. After taking a seat near the designated smoking section, he became extremely angry with the flight attendant who told him to put out his cigarette, because he was not seated in the smoking section that was only one row behind him. This request seemed arbitrary and unreasonable to him.

The airline passenger experienced anger with the accompanying physiological changes: his heart rate changed, his blood pressure rose, and his muscular tension increased.

Rather than considering anger evil or bad, wrong or sinful, anger should be accepted as a completely normal reaction. It is what we do with our anger that can be good or bad, right or wrong.

SUGGESTIONS

The first step is to acknowledge that you are angry and then determine exactly what made you angry. You must define whether you are angry with an employee or still angry at something your spouse did or didn't do at home for example.

Cromey emphasizes that it's our language that often causes trouble on the job. Managers frequently appear to be uncertain or are unclear about the directions they give. The resulting confusion can create frustration among employees that escalates back and forth.

It's better to make direct statements and avoid loaded questions. Don't say: Why isn't that job ready? That can build up resentment. Instead say, I want that job by the end of the day. And then, discuss whether or not that deadline is feasible.

Cromey gives a procedure for expressing anger that he labels as the *RDA Technique: R*—I resent, *D*—I demand, and *A*—I appreciate. Expressing your anger in this order leads to more straightforward communication. For example:

Resent: I don't like the horseplay that goes on around here during lunch.

*D*emand: I expect orderly behavior in the lab at all times.

*A*ppreciate: You are all good technicians; let's keep it on a professional level.

The reason this technique works is that it forces us to label and express the exact behavior that angers us. Employees, as well as friends and children, can change behaviors. But no one knows what to change when just confronted with You make me so angry!

For example, one employee threw his work on the floor and flew into a verbal assault against a client as though the client were there. The manager rushed over and ordered the employee to quiet down and get back to work. The employee then directed his anger toward the manager. Words got stronger and louder. The employee was fired on the spot.

Rightly so, you say? The business lost a skilled 15-year veteran and was compelled to hire an inexperienced recent college graduate as a replacement. Could the manager have handled this outburst differently? Definitely yes.

Let's consider what the manger did wrong. By ordering the employee to quiet down, the manager said, in effect, It's not right to be angry; stop it! That's the last response an angry person will accept.

Now, let's look at another way to handle this situation. First, get the person away from co-workers. Take physical control to protect yourself and others as you sense is necessary. This is one reason for removing the person from the work area.

Next, think of this: Have you ever seen a police officer remove an unruly sports fan from the stands? One reason for doing this is to take away his audience. Often, an angry worker feels she can't back down in front of co-workers, which serves, at best, to delay a resolution to the outburst.

Allow the person to be angry. Your response should portray calm neutrality yet sincere interest. Allow the angry individual to have her say, uninterrupted. To intervene at the outset, as the manger in the example above did, is to run the risk of escalation. Few people will argue with a reasonable, receptive, and empathetic listener.

Anger is a completely normal reaction. It is what we do with anger that can be good or bad, right or wrong.

Then, once the anger has run its course, your response should be one of clarification. Find out all the facts. With whom is the employee angry? What did that person do? In the case described above, was the employee angry at the client or, rather, with the time the complicated task was taking and causing him to fall behind in schedule?

Be specific. When you're sure you understand, restate the problem and reach an agreement on what is at issue. In this way, the person knows that she is understood, and that you are both focused on the problem that caused the anger initially.

Finally, confront the problem. The manager involved in the example above might ask these questions: Is the employee given the same number of jobs as the others, but including *all* the special cases? Should this situation be reassessed? Is the employee overly concerned with the finer points of quality far beyond the industry's or the business's standards? Should this be reexamined?

To reemphasize: Anger results from frustration. An angry person needs to vent negative feelings. You must maintain control of your emotions if you wish an angry employee to eventually regain self-control.

13. When Work Becomes All There Is

Problem:

Am I becoming a workaholic?

Answers:

Acknowledge being addicted to work.

Treat yourself with the same respect you accord to your employees.

Balance work with the other areas of your life.

BACKGROUND

I admit to being a workaholic. There were whole years in my life when I worked 10 or 12-hour days, seven days a week. I took work home with me. I went to my office on Sundays and holidays. If I took a vacation, it was a trip on which I could take enough work to keep me busy. By my early 30s, I had achievement to show for it: advanced degrees, a high-ranking position with an impressive title, and executive's office, and a secretary.

There are legions of workaholics in the work force. Some years ago, futurists saw us working less because of increased uses of new technologies. The reality is just the opposite. More and more of us are working longer and longer hours. We're considered ambitious, goal-oriented, and successful.

But the word *workaholic* is accurate. Like any other addict, I was addicted to work. Work is an addiction when you can't stop putting in those long hours in spite of negative consequences to yourself and your family.

Corporate America is beginning to understand that workaholics are not necessarily its most productive workers.

Workaholics use their formidable energy to complete every task on or before its deadline. They turn idle time into productive time. They seldom delegate, because others cannot meet the standards we have set for ourselves.

Workaholics work with the intensity of a sports competitor. All of one's energy goes into winning. The difference is that a sporting event is a short-lived event—four quarters or five sets and then the competitors go onto other things in their lives. The game the workaholic is playing is 30 or more years long. No one can maintain that intensity without suffering personal consequences.

EXAMPLES

It is true that organizations expect more from their employees today. New technologies didn't reduce the workload; they increased the expectations.

The real explanation, though, is that workaholics use their work and the long hours to avoid dealing with emotions. When you're working you don't have time to deal with your feelings.

Each person experiences the effects of workaholic stress differently. The strain can show in any or all of these categories:

- *Physical.* Being more susceptible to colds and minor infections, high blood pressure, increased heart or breathing rates, upset stomach, teeth grinding, rashes, or exhaustion.
- *Emotional.* Being more prone to anger after small frustrations. For example, slamming down the phone.
- *Mental.* Preoccupation and forgetfulness. Inability to concentrate. Difficulties in making decisions.
- *Behavioral.* Sleep disturbances. An increase in drinking, smoking, or eating, especially junk food.

In California alone, there was a 434 percent increase in stress-related disability claims by state employees in one five-year period.

We can take some tips from executives who handle stress well:

- *Set realistic goals.* If you run into a situation that you can't control, make a decision not to spend a great deal of time on it. Instead, invest your energy in situations where you can be successful.
- *Adapt to change.* Rather than resisting change, find opportunities in change.
- *Develop commitments.* Have a strong personal commitment to your organization and to larger communities.

Some workaholics begin to ask themselves at some point, Is this all there is? Has this been worth the effort? Individuals respond to this crisis differently: Some delay the crisis by turning their attention back to work. Some eventually burn out and become less and less effective. A few face their addiction.

SUGGESTIONS

Just as for other addicts, the first step is awareness— acknowledging that you are addicted to work.

The next step is to begin to respect yourself and treat yourself like you treat others. You wouldn't expect an employee to work 14-hour days. You wouldn't do that to someone you cared about. You have to begin to care about you.

> . . . *workaholics use their work and the long hours to avoid dealing with emotions.*

Some organizations, including AT&T, have adopted weekly "stress-down days" during which employees come to work in jeans and sweatshirts. The effect is relaxing. Other employers, such as Levi Strauss & Co., monitor their managers to insure that they aren't requiring long hours of their employees.

It's critical to plan and schedule rest and recreation into your life. Identify what you consider to be a total break from work. For some it's jogging or golf, for others it's a massage, for others it's shopping. Then schedule these breaks for yourself every day. Don't skip them or cancel them. Breaks are critical to your well-being and improvement. This is the beginning of taking the responsibility to care for yourself.

Another step is to separate work and home. Leave unfinished business at work; don't bring it home and don't feel guilty about leaving work uncompleted. It may help to end the day by making a list of things to do tomorrow—not at home tonight.

Use your commute to unwind. Read or listen to relaxing music. At home, engage in activities that can provide rewards you can't get on the job: gardening, exercise, creative expression, community service.

Finally, discourage phone calls at home from co-workers. The simple question, Can't this wait until tomorrow? quickly ends all but the real emergencies.

Your new objective is to balance your work within your life.

Corporate America is beginning to understand that workaholics are not necessarily its most productive workers. Some companies make it clear that loyalty is not demonstrated by a pattern of long hours. Loyalty is demonstrated by putting in the long hours when seasonal or other reasons demand it.

Jack Welch, chief executive officer of General Electric Co, has said that when someone tells him I'm working 90 hours a week, he says, "You're doing something terribly wrong. I go skiing on the weekend. I go out on Friday. Make a list of 20 things that make you work 90 hours, and 10 of them have to be nonsense."

FOR MORE INFORMATION

Fassel, D. *Working Ourselves to Death: The High Cost of Workaholism, the Rewards of Recovery.* San Francisco, CA: Harper, 1990.

14. Expected Employee Behaviors

Problem:

How do I encourage employees to learn the unwritten rules for success?

Answer:

Be the symbol you want your employees to strive for.

BACKGROUND

Recently, much attention has been given to what have been called *communication rules* or the unwritten expected behaviors appropriate to each situation. If you're driving to Las Vegas and you see a highway patrol car with flashing lights following you, you just know that certain behaviors are expected of you in that situation. You know to pull your car over to the side of the road, you know to wait calmly in your car for the officer to come to you, and you know there is an acceptable way of speaking with the officer. You also know that you don't make fast movements reaching for your glove compartment, and you don't jokingly pretend to be drunk.

In religious services, we recognize certain behaviors as being expected and appropriate. And as a customer in a fancy restaurant, again we are aware that certain behaviors are expected. In each of these cases, the context or the situation has defined the expected appropriate behavior.

The same is true for the workplace. The office situation defines the expected appropriate behavior.

And one thing has become clear: those, who most easily learn the rules, have a much easier time fitting in and being accepted. The term *corporate culture* has been used to describe the unwritten rules of an organization. Each organization has a different corporate culture, because each organization expects slightly different behaviors of its employees.

EXAMPLES

Nonetheless, in Western culture, there are general expected office behaviors common to most businesses.

The October 16, 1988, Sunday newspaper magazine issue of *USA Weekend* asked readers to reply to a survey of office politics.[1] The survey asked readers to identify the unwritten rules about getting ahead at their offices. Thirteen hundred readers wrote back. The top 10 unwritten office rules were reported in their December 11, 1988 issue:

1. Don't rock the boat.
2. Image counts more than hard work.
3. If you don't want the entire office to know, keep it to yourself.
4. Know the secretary well. She's (or he's, I would add) the inside line.
5. Keep smiling—and act as if you know it all.
6. Ignore problems, they'll go away.
7. Do not act smarter than your boss. But be smarter.
8. Don't goof off, that's for the boss only.
9. Let the boss claim the idea.
10. Don't cross the boss.

The term corporate culture is used to describe the unwritten rules at an organization. One thing is clear, those who can more easily learn the rules have a much easier time being accepted.

I asked a college class I instructed to develop their own lists of the unwritten rules at their jobs. The class was composed of people with a wide spectrum of ages and working in a variety of settings.

I then compiled their lists of unwritten rules. Several themes clearly stood out.

• *Appearance.* Many dealt with personal appearance and grooming. One wrote: "Dress like everyone else in the office or better."

• *Use of time.* Many more dealt with the use of time: "Come into work early and do not be in a hurry to leave at the end of the day." Take only proper break time, correct length." "Be willing to work after normal hours." "Schedule personal appointments around work time whenever possible."

• *Attitude.* The most commonly used phrase in this category was "always look busy." One said it this way: "Always look busy. If you have nothing to do, find something. Even if you are only reading, do so with a pencil in hand." Another put it more positively: "Show initiative in generating your own work when times are slack." The other important aspect of attitude was: "Always have a smile." "Try to always be courteous and cheerful to everyone, even when you're in a bad mood." And the standard, yet critical: "The customer is always right."

- *Telephone use.* A good number dealt with the use of the telephone for personal calls. Commonly stated as "No personal calls," one person wrote: "Personal phone calls are usually prohibited. Therefore, if on a personal call and a supervisor approaches, immediately change the subject to a job-related matter. (Your friend on the other end of the line will be thoroughly confused, and this will provide you with some comic relief in an otherwise dull business day!)"

- *Working with co-workers.* Generally the theme was "Respect your fellow workers," which includes such points as: "Don't go through someone else's desk without permission." "Don't talk about other employees' mistakes." "Smoke in designated areas—not in the office." "No sexual remarks to be made in the office." "Never discuss your salary with other employees." "Avoid drinking and eating in the office. Grab a snack on your break." "Take time out to assist new employees." "Try not to inflict your personal problems on other colleagues. There are enough concerns at the office without someone compounding them."

- *Office talk.* The unofficial rules are clear. No profanity and no gossiping. Both should be avoided for personal protection. One wrote: "Don't become involved with office gossip, as you will become a victim if you do."

- *Personal relationships.* Most agreed: "Do not maintain intimate relationships at work." "Do not date co-workers or supervisors." "Be friendly but not intimate with co-workers. With very few, if any, exceptions, keep your private life strictly private."

One wrote about using personal relationships for personal gain: "Do not attempt to sleep your way to the top. There will always be someone better than you waiting in the wings. And there are some ugly bosses out there."

• *Office parties.* Office social events are important: "Attend all social functions related to job." "Watch your behavior at these parties." "Don't get drunk at office parties."

• *Respect for hierarchy.* And finally, the majority of the unwritten office rules dealt with relationships with one's boss: "To your boss, it's always Mr., Ms., or Mrs. Don't call the boss by his or her first name unless instructed to do so." "Never touch your employer." "Talk to your employer with respect." "Don't call the boss at home." "Never say no to your boss. Don't argue with the boss, even if you are right.""When THE big boss comes into the office and wants you, you drop everything and come running." "When leaving an elevator, superiors leave first." "Never precede your superiors when walking together. Walking abreast is reserved for long-time employees. A deferential half-pace behind is recommended." "Talk to your boss first before going to THE boss." "If working with another department, go through the supervisor first." "Know your boss's psychological makeup so you can give him or her the feedback they want to hear." "Let your superiors have all the credit." "The person with the least seniority should answer the telephone first if at all possible." "Do not park in marked parking spaces reserved for someone else." "Do not interrupt superiors. Wait until you've been given that regal, yet almost imperceptible nod of the head, signaling your turn." "Do not go over the boss's head to ask permission for something to which you expect he'll or she'll will oppose." "Do not make important decisions without consulting your boss first."

'To your boss, it's always Mr., Ms., or Mrs. Don't call the boss by his or her first name unless instructed to do so.'

By comparing my students' lists with the *USA Weekend* readers' list, we can see the similarities. My students identified the most important unwritten rule as conform and otherwise respect authority, so you don't get kicked out.

SUGGESTIONS

Corporations have their own argot, their own dress codes, and more importantly, their own values. For most companies, these were established by the personality of the leader: Thomas Watson, Jr. at IBM, Ray Kroc at McDonald's Corp., Walt Disney at Disney Productions, and so on. These were value-shaping leaders with visions to excite thousands of employees.

But each of us serves as a model for our employees. John W Gardner wrote in his book *On Leadership*:[2]

"One function that cannot be delegated is that of serving as symbol. That the leader is a symbol is a fact, not a matter of choice The task is to take appropriate account of that reality and to use it well in the service of the group's goals."

In my national survey of customer service organizations, all of the managers of the most successful businesses stressed how important it is to be a personal model of service. The same applied to each area of office behavior. If you make personal telephone calls at work, you can't expect that your employees won't. If you talk about a client's shortcomings, don't expect that your employees won't. You're their model.

FOR MORE INFORMATION

You'll find many good books on corporate culture. Here's one of the standards:

Deal, T E and A A Kennedy. *Corporate Cultures: The Rites and Rituals of Corporate Life*. Reading, MA: Addison-Wesley Publishing Co., 1982.

15. Business Ethics

Problem:

What can I do to insure my business operates ethically?

Answers:

Top management must continually reinforce that it does not condone illegal acts.

Establish an ethics hot line or confidential advisers to answer questions.

BACKGROUND

In the days of Franklin D Roosevelt or even John F Kennedy, we knew little of our politicians' private lives. The Vietnam War and Watergate scandal resulted in disclosure laws, ethics committees, and policing units as we, the public, continue to expect our politicians to represent higher values. A key issue in the Bush-Clinton campaign was character.

The public's standards are different for athletes and movie stars. For weeks, the press reported allegations of gambling improprieties against Cincinnati Reds manager Pete Rose. A special investigator for the baseball commissioner was said to have evidence that Rose had bet on his own team—an offense punishable by a lifetime ban from baseball. Yet, on the opening day of the baseball season at Riverfront Stadium, banners draped over railings read "Hang in there." Fans gave him a standing ovation. A *New York Times* poll found that only 22 percent of the pubic surveyed had an unfavorable opinion of him.[1] Over half wanted to reserve judgment until they knew more about the allegations. Even after Commissioner A Bartlett Giamatti placed Rose on the ineligible list, permanently banning him from baseball, Rose continued to maintain that he hadn't bet on baseball. The public continues to assume the best of athletes and forgive the worst.

In the 1980s, the movie *Tin Men* showed us the aluminum siding salesmen of a past era who pulled off one outrageous scheme after another on their customers. In the news of the 1980s, we became aware of insider trading scandals, corporate raiders' tactics, and other acts of questionable ethics in the business world, such as Leona Helmsley's evading federal taxes.

Some companies are making more extensive background checks of prospective employees.

Perhaps as a result, an October 1989 Gallup poll showed that only 1 percent of Americans called business ethics very high and 12 percent said they were high. Fifty-four percent said they were average while 29 percent said they were low or very low. About equal numbers of those polled believed that government should play a larger role or that business should do their own housekeeping.[2]

Businesses are responding to this problem. Harvard Business School received its largest gift ever—$23 million—to conduct ethics research. The Harvard Business School now requires its students to take an ethics course.

> . . . only 1 percent of Americans called business ethics very high . . .

The world of business presents us daily with ethical questions in both dealing with customers and dealing with other employees in the organization. Is a secretary wrong to tell a caller that his boss is in a meeting when that is not true? Should you tell a caller that the check is in the mail when it is not? Should a salesperson turn in an expense account that she knows is inflated?

EXAMPLES

According to a study by sociologist Amitai Etzioni, a visiting professor at the Harvard Business School, two-thirds of Fortune 500 companies were convicted over a 10-year period of serious crimes.[3] But remember, companies don't commit crimes, people do. And people can stop illegal activities.

Some companies have developed codes of conduct to guide their employees. Johnson & Johnson, for example, uses its credo statement as the focus for employee training on how to handle everyday situations. To be effective, codes of conduct must be constantly reinforced by management actions.

> . . . all forms of employee theft . . . have been estimated to cost US businesses $50 billion annually.

Hertz Rent a Car was once charged with billing misconduct. The Hertz Corporation rental car customers were
charged retail repair rates that were higher than the dis-
counted rates Hertz paid for those repairs. While this continues to be a general practice in the rental car industry,
Hertz discontinued the practice. Hertz top executives
started visiting every one of their offices on a regular basis
to reinforce that Hertz has no tolerance for misconduct.

In a speech given to the Orange County (California)
Travel and Transportation Council and the Greater Los
Angeles Travel and Transportation Council in 1988, chairman and chief executive officer of the Hertz Corporation,
Frank Olson, emphasized that the single most important
influence on employee ethics is the example set by the chief
executive and other top executives: "The best guarantee that
employees will make those decisions ethically is to create an
environment in which the employee will know how management would expect him or her to act."

US citizens are becoming increasingly active in demand-
ing that companies be good citizens. Consumers have with-
held business from companies that invest in South Africa,
from companies with a record of environmental pollution
or hazardous products, from companies that advertise on
offensive television programs, and from companies charged
with testing products on animals.

Some consumers intentionally buy Campbell's Prego spaghetti sauce over Unilever's Ragu spaghetti sauce because
Campbell's runs a day care center or because Unilever in-
vests in South Africa.

SUGGESTIONS

What guidelines can we turn to for guidance in making daily
ethical decisions? The ethical tradition places the greatest
importance on the individual's responsibilities to society as

a whole. In an ethical society, we all have an obligation to keep promises and to tell the truth. And right and wrong don't change when we enter the world of business.

Some people in the world of business will say that it's not all that black and white: Telling little lies, for example, simply goes with the territory—no one is getting hurt. Give bosses the benefit of the doubt. You don't know all the facts.

Others recommend facing the more serious ethical questions: If you are told to do an illegal act, explain in a professional manner that you believe what you have been asked to do is illegal and because of that you do not wish to do it. If the response is, Do it or else, you still have alternatives.

If the company is basically ethical, consider going over your superior's head. If the company itself is acting unethically, look out for yourself and leave the company.

If you're fired because you refused to perform an illegal act, officially notify the company's personnel office. In some states you have legal recourse: Employees who are asked to perform an illegal act and are then fired for failing to comply can sue for damages.

You are the only one who can decide if you want to work for someone who is unethical.

Have you ever taken a ream of paper or a box of paper clips home from the office? Have you ever used the office phone to make personal long distance calls? We don't think of ourselves as criminals for doing these things, but in reality any unlawful or dishonest act that costs the company money is employee theft.

Employees don't tend to think of petty theft as a crime. It's even often thought of as an unofficial job perquisite. But all forms of employee theft, from paper clips to embezzlement, have been estimated to cost US businesses *$50 billion* annually.

What can be done to prevent employee theft and other forms of misconduct? Some companies are making more extensive background checks of prospective employees.

Some are tightening their internal audit and inspection procedures, while still others are encouraging employees to report dishonesty among co-workers. But whatever is done, it must be constantly reinforced by top management.

Ethics hot lines are one way of helping to determine what's appropriate behavior. Recently some large employers, particularly defense companies, have set up the hot lines to help stop problems before they grow too large. While the trend is too new to determine if hot lines are worth the expense, the hope is that they will help avoid litigation, fines, suspensions, and disbarments.

St. Louis-based General Dynamics Corporation was one of the first defense firms to set up an ethics hot line in 1985. Its Pomona Division, which had about 6,600 employees, received about 20 calls a month on its hot line. Its Valley Systems Division, which had about 3,300 employees, reported an average of 15 calls a month.

Calls are handled by the company's own ethics specialists or attorneys. The most commonly asked questions tend to deal with conflicts of interest and billing. Calls are kept confidential except for information regarding security breaches or illegal conduct, which are reported to authorities. Companywide, General Dynamics imposed 205 sanctions in one year originating from hot line calls. Violations reported ranged from billing the company for overtime not worked to accepting gifts from suppliers to falsifying test results. Penalties ranged from warnings to firings.

FOR MORE INFORMATION

More and more books are appearing recently on business ethics. Here's one you can consult:

Guy, M E. *Ethical Decision Making in Everyday Work Situations.* Westport, CN: Quorum Books, 1990.

RELATIONS WITH EMPLOYEES

16. Employment Interviewing

Problem:

Just what can I ask a job applicant in an interview?

Answers:

First decide what information you need to know.
Devise questions that probe in those areas.
Develop a strong interview introduction.

BACKGROUND

Recently, I eavesdropped on a manager interviewing a prospective employee. To my surprise, the interview lasted no more than 10 minutes. After the applicant had left, I asked the manager for his evaluation of the applicant.

"He wouldn't be happy here," the manager replied. I asked how he had reached that decision so quickly. The manager explained that he had discovered in the interview that the candidate lived in another town some 60 miles away and would face a two-hour daily commute. His experience was that employees who commuted would leave the job when they were able to find another closer to home.

In 10 minutes, this manager avoided a costly hiring mistake. He did it by knowing in advance what to ask and how to ask it.

EXAMPLES

Professional employment interviewers are thoroughly prepared. As a result, they are in control of the interview and are most likely to get the information they need to make a sound decision. Being in control of the interview includes controlling the setting and starting out clearly.

Give attention to planning where the interview will be conducted. If you maintain a casual relationship with your employees, approach the interview in a casual manner.

On the other hand, if you maintain a formal relationship with your employees, then by all means conduct the interview in a formal setting, such as in a private office.

Arrange to prevent visits and telephone calls from interrupting the interview. Ask the applicant to sit in a chair opposite you or at the side of the desk.

Before you ask the first question, you need to establish rapport, orientation, and motivation.

Rapport

Job applicants may be nervous or present themselves as overconfident. Your objective is to have a pleasant conversation that also yields useful information.

You can gain rapport through simple human courtesies, such as giving a friendly greeting, offering coffee, and talking about the weather, the news, or another comfortable topic, before moving on.

Orientation

Job applicants will also be more relaxed if you provide clear orientation; that is, if you describe what will be covered in the interview.

For example, when I explain to a job applicant that the interview will last an hour and that during that hour we will be reviewing items on her written application, the applicant tends to feel more at ease to talk.

Motivation

Finally, even in employment interviews, some motivation is necessary. You get more information if you explain why it is in the best interest of the applicant to be as complete and accurate as possible.

SUGGESTIONS

First decide in which areas you need information about the applicant. Next think about how to get that information with your questions. Finally, give some thought to the order of your questions. Generally, you want to start with the more open-ended questions and end with the more direct and perhaps even more threatening questions.

The following is an open-ended question: What do you think is the best working relationship between a manager and an employee?

The direct question, What salary do you expect? should be asked at the end of the interview. If asked this first, the applicant may continue to justify that amount in answers to all subsequent questions.

The most common, and probably the best procedure is to spend the first 60 to 70 percent of the interview discussing the applicant, and the last 30 to 40 percent discussing the company and the job.

Today there is some legal pressure for the employer to cover the same areas with every applicant at every interview for the available job. Although there are some 25 different governmental agencies that share control over discrimination, there are no universal legal restraints imposed on the selection activity.

Restraints include court decisions, federal laws, state laws, local laws, and your company's own affirmative action plans. But most of the laws have exceptions; they may not apply to you. For example, the Age Discrimination Act only covers organizations of more than 20 employees.

In 10 minutes, this manager avoided a costly hiring mistake. He did it by knowing in advance what to ask and how to ask it.

I'm not giving legal advice by providing the following list of topics to avoid. I'm only suggesting that today these areas are generally considered inappropriate or illegal in employment interviews:

- Race.
- Age.
- Religion.
- Marital status.
- National origin.

- Holidays observed.
- Original name.
- Length of time in the United States.
- Citizenship of relatives.
- Current or anticipated pregnancy status.
- Credit standing.
- Spouse's occupation.
- Anticipated length of time working.
- Views of feminism or civil rights.
- Type of military discharge.
- Membership in organizations, clubs, lodges, fraternities.
- Arrest record (you can ask if the applicant has ever been convicted and if yes, for details).
- Languages known (you can ask if this is a bona fide employment qualification).

The answer to the question what to do with the answers? is to always remember to probe for additional information no matter how good the answer sounds at first.

Remember, research and the experiences of professional employment interviewers show that planned interviews cover information more consistently and are therefore more reliable.

> [R]esearch and the experiences of professional employment interviewers show that planned interviews cover information more consistently and are therefore more reliable.

What do you need to know? An American Management Association's publication, *Selection of Management Personnel*, suggests that you need information in at least three areas:[1] educational background, work experience, and personal factors, such as career goals and objectives. It's a good idea to list these areas first.

Next, decide how to phrase questions so you will get the information you need. One tip: avoid asking closed-ended questions that can be answered with a simple yes or no. They don't give you much information. Instead, use:

- Direct questions that ask for specific information.
- Indirect questions that get at the information from a different angle.
- Open-ended questions that encourage longer answers.

For example, rather than asking, Did you get along with your former employer? you can get more information with a direct question, such as: How did you get along with your former employer?; or an indirect question, such as Were I to check, what do you think your former employer would say about you?

"Probe" questions are not planned; they are the follow-up questions asked in response to the information the applicant volunteers. Remember to probe analytically and thoroughly. Research has shown that most interviewers believe what they are told and are manipulated by the applicant.

For example, at one interview, every time the manager asked about the applicant's current job, the applicant talked at length about how much she enjoyed working with her hands.

Actually, the applicant had a job in which she was very unhappy. She deliberately avoided saying this, because she was afraid an admission that she had problems would be judged negatively by the manager. Probe questions would have opened up that area.

Generally, the interviewer needs to do two things at the end of the interview:

1. Simply review what was covered in the interview. This gives the applicant a chance to verify that you have the correct information.

2. Indicate to the applicant what the next step will be. Telling the applicant to expect to hear from you again after two weeks prevents many unsolicited telephone inquiries.

It's the recommended general practice today not to tell an applicant at the interview that he will not be hired. It is preferable to explain to the applicant by letter that someone else more closely met the job requirements.

To be in control of the interview includes controlling the setting and starting out clearly.

Finally, there are two other tips I'd like to pass on that apply no matter how large or small a business you have. In the long term, it never pays to misrepresent any aspect of the job or company to an applicant (it causes bad public relations at the least). And always document, for your files, your conversation with an applicant. You never know when you might be called upon to justify your decision.

We all want good employees, and most of us make our hiring decisions on the basis of employment interviews. With a little preparation time for the interview, we are more likely to get the information we need to make those critical hiring decisions.

FOR MORE INFORMATION

There are many good interviewing guides. Here's one:

Smart, B D. *The Smart Interviewer.* New York, NY: Wiley, 1989.

17. Employee Morale

Problem:

How can I improve employee morale?

Answers:

Find out what really is valued by employees.
Recognize that morale is tied to turnover.

BACKGROUND

Management concern about employee job satisfaction dates back at least to the late 1920s when Harvard University's Elton Mayo and his colleagues became convinced that workers would work harder if they were happier.

At the Hawthorne Works of Western Electric near Chicago, management experimented with the effects of lighting and discovered that increases in lighting improved work performance. But to their surprise, when management later reduced the lighting, efficiency didn't decrease!

Job satisfaction does not seem to be a clear cause of absenteeism.

After another study at the plant, researchers concluded that the workers were motivated to work hard and well, because they felt special having been singled out for these research projects, (that is, management considered workers important). Another reason was the employees had already developed good relationships with one another and with their supervisor. It is now generally agreed that actual working conditions are less important to job satisfaction than employees' feelings that management is concerned about them.

This gives meaning to the phrase, *Hawthorne effect*. If workers are singled out for special attention, they tend to perform better.

Operating with the assumption that the satisfied worker produces more, managers and researchers have for years tried to determine exactly what makes workers satisfied. In fact, by the mid-1970s at least 3,000 research studies had been published. Job requirements, pay, supervision, promotions, co-workers, and myriad other factors have been shown to affect job satisfaction.

It remains true to this day that changes in job satisfaction have seldom been shown to affect production in any dramatic way. Satisfaction with work and productivity are not necessarily related. Indeed, it has often been said that dissatisfied workers can be creative or can at least perform the job as well as a satisfied worker. And job satisfaction does not seem to be a clear cause of absenteeism.

So why be concerned about keeping workers satisfied? Although other factors do play a part, job dissatisfaction has been shown to affect turnover. One estimate for the average cost of resignation, hiring, and training is $2,500 (the range being $1,500 to $12,000), so employee turnover can definitely affect profitability.

And, job satisfaction has been shown, even more clearly, to affect counterproductive behavior, such as sabotage on the job. Examples include doing work poorly or incorrectly on purpose; spreading rumors or gossip to cause trouble at work; damaging employer's property, equipment, or product on purpose; stealing employer's property; and using alcohol or drugs on the job.

Although other factors do play a part, job dissatisfaction has been shown to affect turnover. One estimate for the average cost of resignation, hiring, and training is $2,500 . . . so employee turnover can definitely affect profitability.

Good employee job satisfaction can save the employer the cost of turnover and counterproductive behavior.

EXAMPLES

We've all heard and read how service workers are dissatisfied. It has become an accepted truism that service workers hate their jobs. I recently conducted a nationwide survey of customer service workers' job satisfaction. We can look at these results as examples of ways to improve employee morale and of how morale is tied to turnover.

Let's look at the figures.

To the question, "How proud are (were) you of what you do (did) for a living?," with 1 being "extremely proud" and

5 being "not at all proud" the average was 2.5—on the proud side.

To the question,"How well does (did) this job match your skills?," with 1 being "extremely well" and 5 being "not at all," the average was 2.7—again on the positive side.

To the question, "Is this the job your family or parents want (wanted) you to have?," with 1 being "they are very satisfied" and 5 being "they are very dissatisfied," the average was 2.8—again on the positive side.

To the question, "How important do you think your job is (was) compared with other jobs?," with 1 being "very important" and 5 being "not at all important," the average was 2.5—clearly on the important side.

To the question, "How important do people think your job is (was) compared with other jobs?," with 1 being "very important" and 5 being "not at all important," the average was 2.7—again on the positive side.

Then to the direct question, "How satisfied are you with your current (or most recent) service job?," with 1 being "very satisfied" and 5 being "very dissatisfied," the average of 2.6 was clearly on the positive side. Table 17-1 shows a breakdown on the responses to this question.

To look at the effect on expectations, I asked, Is (Was) your job as satisfying as you originally expected it to be?, with 1 being "yes, as satisfying" and 5 being "no, not as satisfying," the average was a positive 2.6.

Overall, all of these seem to confirm that service workers are satisfied with their jobs. To confirm this, I also asked about changing jobs.

I think the evidence shows that service workers are satisfied.

To the question, If you had a choice to do something else, would you stay in your current or most recent service job?, service workers could select one of the following five choices:

1. I'd do anything else.
2. I'd do something different and better.

TABLE 17-1
Responses to the Question, How satisfied are you with your current (or most recent) service job?

Satisfaction Level	Percentage
1 (very satisfied)	19.9
2	32.7
3	26.3
4	14.1
5 (very dissatisfied)	7.0

3. I'd do something sort-of like what I'm doing now.

4. I'd do something similar and better.

5. I'd stay where I am.

The results:

7.0 percent would stay where they are.

7.2 percent would do something like what they're doing now.

29.1 percent would do something similar and better.

52.5 percent would do something different and better.

Only 4.2 percent would do anything else.

SUGGESTIONS

I think the evidence shows that service workers are satisfied. But, do you as a manager know what contributes to service worker job satisfaction?

Take the following test:

Rank the following five items. Rank *first* the item you believe service workers report as most important to them in determining how satisfied they feel with their jobs. Then rank the remainder according to importance.

_____ Expressing concern and warm feelings for others.
_____ Having freedom and independence at work.
_____ Knowing you are doing a service for others.
_____ Receiving respect from others.
_____ Earning salary and benefits.

Number one according to my survey is freedom. Service workers expect to have the authority to make decisions on the job themselves. Freedom was followed by respect, salary and benefits, expression of concern, and knowledge that you are doing a service job in that order.

I need to add another touch to the overall picture. Remember that most service workers wanted to change jobs—some to something similar, others to something different. People dream about the future, and for most of us, those dreams of the future are of a world better than our experiences of the present. Service workers are not exceptions to this rule.

Service workers who feel more management encouragement to report customer reactions and ideas tend to be more satisfied.

To the question, "Is (was) this the job you think you belong in?", with 1 being "exactly where I should be," and 5 being "I really don't belong here," the average response was 3.4.

To the question, "Is (was) this the job you always wanted to have—the one you dreamed of doing?", with 1 being "exactly what I wanted" and 5 being "opposite of what I wanted," the average was 3.6.

And finally to the question, "Is this a job you could be satisfied with five years later?", with 1 being "extremely satisfied" and 5 being "not at all satisfied," the average was 3.8.

Who are the more satisfied service workers? In my survey they were older, college educated people in high paying jobs. Service workers who must deal directly with customers whose expectations of service are different from what they will receive, are less satisfied with their jobs. Service

TABLE 17-2
Percent Agreeing with the Statement

	More Satisfied	Less Satisfied
Stay where they are.	12.1%	1.9%
Do something similar to what they're doing now.	7.9	6.7
Do something similar and better.	41.5	8.7
Do something different and better.	37.0	72.1
Do anything else.	1.5	10.6

workers who feel more management encouragement to report customer reactions and ideas tend to be more satisfied. Service workers, who feel more authority to solve customer complaints on the spot tend to be more satisfied. And, those service workers who have received more training and more information on how their organization is unique also tend to be more satisfied.

I can also add that the more satisfied service workers tend to have a higher opinion of themselves and to view customers, people in general, and themselves as more pleasant. They also report preferring service work over management and manufacturing.

But, does a concern for employee job satisfaction pay off? Does my survey show that relationship between job satisfaction and turnover? It does. See Table 17-2. The more satisfied service employees are six to seven times more likely to stay on the job than the less satisfied service employees are.

18. Avoiding Groupthink

Problem:

What can I do to avoid the negative side effects of team spirit?

Answers:

In the groups you lead, set a climate that encourages people to think and express themselves critically.

Balance team spirit and competition.

BACKGROUND

The main theme of Yale University psychologist Irving L Janis's book *Victims of Groupthink* came to him while reading Arthur M Schlesinger's chapters on the Bay of Pigs invasion in *A Thousand Days*[1] How could John F Kennedy and his advisers have made such poor decisions? Janis was struck with how group dynamics had interfered with effective decision making.

> *. . . groupthink is widespread in business as well as government.*

To learn more about this, he studied four major fiascoes resulting from poor decisions made during the administrations of four American presidents—Franklin D Roosevelt (failure to be prepared for the attack on Pearl Harbor), Harry S Truman (the invasion of North Korea), John F Kennedy (the Bay of Pigs invasion), and Lyndon B Johnson (escalation of the Vietnam War). For comparative purposes, he also studied two examples of carefully worked out decisions made by similar groups—Harry S Truman (the Marshall Plan) and John F Kennedy (the Cuban missile crisis).

Janis's findings have direct application to all of us who work in organizations. Year after year, we hear of collective miscalculations, companies gone bankrupt because of misjudging their markets, federal agencies making costly mistakes. Why do these bad decisions occur? Janis's findings give us an answer.

Group identification and feelings of solidarity are labeled by psychologists as *cohesiveness.* Many managers encourage group identification and feelings of solidarity to get that team spirit they believe is necessary to increase productivity or sales.

While that may be true, Janis calls our attention to the *negative consequences* of team spirit. Team spirit often demands consensus at any cost. That, in turn, suppresses dissent and appraisal of alternatives. In decision-making groups, the result is often disastrously poor decisions.

Janis coined the word *groupthink* to refer to the phenomenon that occurs in highly cohesive groups when group members, striving for unanimity, override their need to realistically appraise alternative courses of action.

EXAMPLES

Janis makes it clear that groupthink is widespread in business as well as government. Some infamous historical examples will illustrate:

In 1956, the directors of Ford Motor Co decided to introduce the medium-priced Edsel despite mounting evidence that the public wanted low-priced cars. Ford directors dismissed the accelerating sales of foreign cars as "the teacher trade," or a small or insignificant market with little potential for profit. The Edsel resulted in a net loss of more than $300 million.

In 1961, the directors and scientists of Grunenthal Chemie ignored reports from physicians all over the world and advertised the drug thalidomide as safe enough to be used by pregnant women even though the firm had not conducted a single test to study the drug's effects on the fetus. Within a year, approximately 7,000 deformed children were born of mothers on the drug. The firm paid out millions in damages.

> . . . the group leader needs to carefully balance team spirit and healthy competition.

With just these two examples, anyone can see that the list of fiascoes continues today. Janis further suggests that if decisions made by any single, policy-making group in government, industry, medicine, law, education, or other fields are examined carefully, a sizable percentage of errors would prove to be attributable to groupthink.

Janis identifies eight symptoms of groupthink. Watch for these same symptoms in your organization:

1. *Illusion of invulnerability.* When shared by most or all of the members of a decision-making group, an illusion of invulnerability creates excessive optimism and encourages the taking of extreme risks. Janis uses as an example the belief that Pearl Harbor was invulnerable which left the United States unprepared for the Japanese attack.

2. *Shared stereotypes.* Stereotypical views of the opposition's leaders as either too evil to warrant genuine negotiation attempts or too weak and stupid to counter whatever risky attempts are made to defeat them are more symptoms. Janis uses the example of the US crossing of the 38th parallel in disregard of Chinese warnings. The US decision-makers held a shared stereotype of the Chinese as being controlled by Russia and not able to act unilaterally.

3. *Rationalization.* Collective rationalizations are used to discount warnings that might lead the members to reconsider their assumptions before they recommit themselves to their past policy decisions.

4. *The illusion of morality.* An unquestioned belief in the group's inherent morality inclines members to ignore the ethical or moral consequences of their decisions.

5. *Self-censorship.* Self-censorship of deviations from apparent group consensus reflects each member's inclination to rationalize the importance of doubts and counterarguments.

6. *Illusion of unanimity.* A shared illusion of unanimity about judgments conforming to the majority view. Janis refers to Arthur Schlesinger's discounting his own doubts about the Bay of Pigs decision because of feelings that voicing those doubts would affect the unanimity of the group. Later, Schlesinger discovered that others involved in that decision also had doubts they did not voice out of the same fear.

7. *Direct pressure.* Direct pressure on any member who expresses strong opposition to any of the group's stereotypes, illusions, or commitments, making clear that this type of dissent is contrary to what is expected of all loyal members.

8. *Mind guarding.* The emergence of self-appointed mind guards—members who protect the group from adverse information that might shatter shared complacency about the effectiveness and morality of their decisions. Bodyguards protect one's body; mind guards protect minds from disturbing ideas.

SUGGESTIONS

As I conduct seminars across the country on conflict management and negotiation, I often describe Janis's ideas to illustrate how conflict in an organization is helpful to the organization. That is, it is through open conflict over ideas and alternatives that better decisions are reached. Organizations need to encourage that type of conflict to avoid groupthink.

Many, many people, though, tell me that groupthink characterizes their organization and they ask me what they, as middle-managers, can do. I tell them that realistically it is the top-level manager who establishes the culture of the organization—and that includes setting the climate for groupthink or for healthy conflict over ideas and alternatives.

Each of us, though, leads some group and each of us can set the climate for that group.

Groupthink can be prevented. Based on Janis's prescriptions, I provide my seminar groups with the following ways to prevent groupthink and improve the quality of their group's decisions:

1. Establish an atmosphere where people will be free to raise appropriate objections.

2. Care should be taken not to define the expected results.

3. Set up parallel, independent policy-making groups.

4. If personnel is limited, periodically divide the policy-making group into two or more subgroups.

5. Have group representatives act as information liaisons with their factions.

6. Independent outside expects should be invited in to challenge the views of the core members.

7. Encourage the role of a devil's advocate.

8. Try to think like the competition.

9. Before ratifying any decisions, a second meeting should be held to express any residual doubts and to rethink the issue.

Finally, the group leader needs to carefully balance team spirit and healthy competition. With too much team spirit, we get the negative effects of groupthink. With too much competition, we get the effects of nonproductive conflict. The leader needs people who can work together but who also feel free to raise appropriate objections.

FOR MORE INFORMATION

In this case, the original reference is the best:

Janis, I L. *Victims of Groupthink.* Boston: MA Houghton Mifflin Company, 1972.

19. Ethnic Diversity in the Workforce

Problem:

How can I prepare my workforce for more immigrant employees?

Answers:

Assist the recent immigrant in learning English.

Build a team identity that overrides individual differences.

BACKGROUND

For the first time ever, the 1980 US census questionnaire asked Americans to volunteer their ethnic origin. Ten percent didn't answer. Of the remaining 90 percent, a full 83 percent identified with an ethnic group. Only six percent refused ethnic labeling by referring to themselves as Americans.

The American melting pot of old included English, German, Irish, French, and Italian immigrants and encouraged ethnic uniformity. A patriotic significance was placed on learning English and becoming American.

In more recent history between 1952 and 1965, the US government did not encourage immigration. During the 1970s, however, an average one-half million immigrants entered the country legally each year. The 1980s was the second largest immigration decade in US history. It's estimated that the 1990s will be the largest. There are now *50 ethnic groups* with sizable populations in the United States.[1]

Thus, today's immigrants find a much more ethnically diversified America. In some areas, people of similar ethnic origin reside together in large subcommunities. These more recent immigrants experience less pressure to immediately learn fluent English and become "Americanized" than did their predecessors.

The number of people in the United States whose chosen, or first, language is one other than English rose from 28 million in 1976 to 34.7 million in 1990. That number is projected to reach 39.5 million by the year 2000. The number of people for whom Spanish is the chosen, or first, language will rise from 10.6 million (38 percent of the total) in 1976 to 18.2 million (46 percent) by the year 2000. These numbers make the United States the fifth-largest Hispanic nation in the world.

EXAMPLES

At a large Los Angeles bank with employees from many ethnic groups, managers began to notice that on coffee and lunch breaks, workers from the same ethnic background consistently sat together.

The managers recognized that it was on those breaks and lunches that employees discussed their jobs and the organization. Moreover, they recognized that such social separations did nothing to enhance an overriding identity for the company. It may have, in fact, served to segregate what should have been a team organization. Management soon decided that it was in the company's interest to actively stimulate acculturation for immigrant workers.

. . . not one of us can claim to be completely free of prejudice.

Besides suggesting continued education, managers anywhere can encourage new immigrant workers to spend time with co-workers in an effort to become more involved. Managers might also remind the company's old-timers of the importance of socializing with the new workers for the enrichment of all concerned. Creating a comfortable environment in the company, where cross-communication and camaraderie are encouraged, is a less direct step for managers to take, but one that can certainly be effective and well-received.

At this same Los Angeles bank, an Asian immigrant was fired for just cause. She did not dispute her firing, but asked permission to return to the bank in order to apologize personally to every other employee of her ethnic background. It was her belief that she had failed her group. Her values placed much emphasis on a responsibility to group membership, but also illustrated a sense of security within and loyalty to that group that she did not feel with other members of the organization.

There are now 50 ethnic groups *with sizable populations in the United States.*

Using the broad definition, not one of us can claim to be completely free of prejudice. We like and respond well to some people and not others. While most identify the word as applying to reactions to obvious personal attributes such as race, creed, or color, prejudice often arises from much more subtle interactions—many of them unintentional or subconscious. Prejudice entering into employment activities represents one variety of *discrimination.* Prejudice among co-workers is another concern for any business.

In the Los Angeles bank referred to earlier, there was, in fact, an excellent affirmative action hiring policy. Nonetheless, ethnic group members employed there complained about more subtle, and perhaps unconscious, prejudice.

For example, they noticed that a white male manager spent extra time explaining how the bank *really* works to his protege—another young white male who had attended the same school as the manager. This information was not shared with any ethnic employees.

In another instance, a white female department manager posted training opportunities as required, but strongly encouraged other white women in the department to sign up. She never mentioned these opportunities to males or any ethnic group members.

This *unconscious prejudice* is, of course, difficult to avoid. I think the best way to address the problem is to *state the criteria for every personnel action.* For example, if you can afford to send only one staff member to a particular training program, establish the criteria for your selection before making a choice that would otherwise seem to suggest partiality. Award the opportunity to a senior employee, to the employee with the quarter's most outstanding production record, or on a first-come, first-served basis, for example.

SUGGESTIONS

Unlike a temporary visitor, the immigrant immediately must find a new source of livelihood and build a new life. This process is called *acculturation*.[2] We seldom think of those of English, German, Irish, French or Italian descent as ethnic groups, because through successive generations, these groups have become assimilated into a somewhat homogenized society.

No immigrant, as long as livelihood needs must be met in a new country, can escape acculturation. Individuals do differ, however, as to what degree they become acculturated.

For example, an immigrant from Canada to the United States finds the process of acculturation easier than a Vietnamese immigrant. There can also be differences among immigrants from the same country—depending upon, for example, whether they grew up in a cosmopolitan urban center or a rural area with little Western influence. Younger immigrants adapt more easily than older ones. Educational background and personality can also determine how readily immigrants will desire to blend in with a new culture. Finally, previous travel, contact with overseas friends or family, and mass media influence also come into play.

The key to ensuring health, job satisfaction, and productivity for an employed new immigrant is understanding how acculturated the worker is and to encourage the employee's involvement as a true team member within your organization.

If the employee is far into the acculturation process, there will be few, if any, communication or social problems resulting from ethnic background. Such problems are potential, however, for the newly immigrated worker who is just beginning the process.

An employee who seems relatively noncommunicative, for example, may be experiencing language difficulties. In such a case, both manager and co-workers should be sensitive to the need for clear directions and other communications.

Don't simply ask, Do you understand? at the end of a direction or comment. Any employee anxious to please you will say yes, regardless of whether or not the message was completely clear.

Instead, explain at the start that you understand the difficulties of learning a new language and that you encourage the employee to ask questions whenever something is unclear. After establishing this support, the employee should not feel uncomfortable repeating back your directions during initial training phases. If language is a greater problem than you anticipated at hiring, you might refer the employee to an English as a second language course. Available at a local school or community college, this course can help accelerate the worker's understanding of English and ease initial difficulties.

Today, managers must learn to cope with ethnic diversity. The melting pot is gone; America now is experiencing ethnic diversity. Understanding this diversity and encouraging *another* group identity—namely, the team identity of your business, united toward the same goal—can enable personal diversities to enhance, rather than detract from, internal rapport, job satisfaction, and a productive and successful business.

FOR MORE INFORMATION

Roosevelt, Jr., T R, "From Affirmative Action to Affirming Diversity." *Harvard Business Review,* March–April, 1990, pp. 107–117.

Gardenswartz L and A Rowe. *Managing Diversity: A Complete Desk Reference and Planning Guide.* Homewood, Il: Business One Irwin, 1993.

20. Dealing with Alcoholism

Problem:

How should I deal with an employee with a drinking problem?

Answers:

Develop a written policy on alcoholism.

Document the effects on the employee's job performance.

Refer the employee to assistance programs.

BACKGROUND

Cover stories of both *Time* magazine and *U.S. News & World Report* have featured alcoholism. Why the concern? Two court cases may explain: Michael Deaver, a former aide to President Ronald Reagan, used alcoholism as a defense in his trial for lying to a grand jury, and two former soldiers sought to overturn a half-century old Veterans Administration policy that classifies alcoholism as "willful misconduct" rather than as a sickness.

Nonetheless, the statistics quoted in news stories are startling:

- Two out of every three high school seniors have drunk alcohol within the past month. Five percent drink daily. Forty percent of sixth graders have tasted wine coolers.
- Two of every three adults drink. But only 10 percent of the nation's drinkers consume half of its beer, wine, and liquor. The South and the West have the most abstainers, but their drinkers drink the most.
- Nearly 18 million adults in the United States are problem drinkers. More than 10 million of these are suffering from alcoholism.
- One family in four has been troubled by alcohol—the highest incidence of problem drinking in a Gallup Poll shows a trend that dates back to 1950.[1]

As far back as 1957, the American Medical Association (AMA) has defined alcoholism as a disease. It is officially defined as "an illness characterized by preoccupation with alcohol and loss of control over its consumption such as to lead usually to intoxication if drinking is begun, by chronicity, by progression, and by tendency toward relapse."

The overwhelming majority of people agree with the AMA. A recent Gallup Poll found 87 percent of those interviewed endorsed the concept of alcoholism as a disease.[2]

EXAMPLES

Ashton Brisolara, executive director of the Committee on Alcoholism and Drug Abuse for Greater New Orleans, estimates that alcoholism affects five percent of the workforce. He writes that the alcoholic employee is absent 22 more days per year than the nonalcoholic employee.[3]

What signs should alert the supervisor? Brisolara gives a list of clues that might indicate problems:

- Absenteeism.
- Temporary departures from the job.
- Unusual excuses.
- Mood changes.
- Red or bleary eyes.
- Low quality of work.
- Loud talking.
- Drinking at lunch.
- Long breaks.
- Rapid drinking.
- Suspiciousness.
- Tremors.
- Excessive nervousness.
- Increased tolerance for alcohol.
- Denial.
- Spasmodic work pace.
- Lower quantity of work.
- Hangovers on the job.
- Breath purifiers.
- Financial problems.
- Depressed condition.
- Drinking on the job.
- Avoidance of supervisors and workers.

- Flushed face.
- Increased occurrence of minor illnesses.
- Family problems.
- Resentfulness.
- Losing tools and materials.
- Neglecting details.

Nothing on this list is proof of alcoholism. Nevertheless, lower job performance along with these signs is reason to talk with the employee.

SUGGESTIONS

No matter the size of your company, you need to be prepared to take steps.

Every business should have a written policy concerning alcoholism. There is a high degree of consistency among current alcoholism policy statements. Most businesses prohibit alcohol use on the job. Most clearly state that alcoholism is a treatable illness and that accepting treatment for alcoholism will in no way jeopardize the employee's future career, although refusal to accept treatment will leave the employee open to usual disciplinary procedures for substandard job performance. Finally, most policies state that any record of participation in an alcoholism program will be treated as confidential medical information.

A Conference Board report gave the following excerpt from an alcoholism policy as a model: ''For the purpose of this policy, alcoholism is defined as an illness in which an employee's consumption of any alcoholic beverage definitely and repeatedly interferes with his or her job performance and health.[4]''

Supervisors are not expected to make a medical diagnosis but should make referrals strictly on the basis of an unsatisfactory job performance that seems to result from an apparent behavioral medical problem in a previously competent worker.

When you document an employee, again the emphasis should be on job performance. Before approaching the employee, document the absences and the reduced quality and quantity of work. At all times the discussion should center on performance.

Experience has shown that repeated lectures, second, third, and fourth chances, and offers of help simply don't work. The key has been constructive use of the supervisor's authority. The alcoholic employee must be made to understand that unless the problem is corrected and performance is brought up to standard, the employee will be subject to existing penalties for unsatisfactory job performance. The employee must also understand that acceptance of treatment will not jeopardize employment or opportunity for promotion.

Since alcoholism occurs in every business, takes a toll on productivity, and is increasingly viewed as a disease, more and more employers have organized alcoholism programs. Employee Assistance Programs, as they are now called, exist in some form in most businesses today. Most of these programs are based on the job performance approach. It is on the job that the symptoms of lateness, absenteeism, and lowered job performance show up. Employers are in the best position to motivate an alcoholic to accept treatment because the threat of losing one's job is the most effective motivation for getting the alcoholic to treatment. Sometimes called constructive confrontation, the employee is basically told to shape up or expect to be fired.

No one has found conclusive answers on which type of treatment is best for which type of alcoholic. First check what treatment your employee health plan covers. Most insurance plans favor in-patient treatment in a hospital, although some pay for residential care or out-patient programs.

Overall, the most highly accepted form of treatment is Alcoholics Anonymous (AA). With some 676,000 members, AA is considered to be the single most effective means of helping the alcoholic. A donation of $1 or $2 per person per meeting is customary for coffee and doughnuts, but the program is free.

FOR MORE INFORMATION

Alcoholics Anonymous
PO Box 459
Grand Central Station
New York, NY 10163
(212) 870-3400

Employee Assistance Professionals Association
4601 North Fairfax Drive
Suite 1001
Arlington, VA 22203
(703) 522-6272

National Clearinghouse for Alcohol and Drug Information
PO Box 2345
Rockville MD 20847
(301) 468-2600 or (800) 729-6686
Extensive lists of treatment programs as well as information on specific alcohol and drug problems.

National Council on Alcoholism and Drug Dependence
12 West 21st Street
New York, NY 10010
(800) NCA-CALL

National Institute on Drug Abuse—the Drug-free Workplace Helpline
(800) 843-4971

21. Performance Evaluation

Problem:

How should I evaluate employee performance?

Answers:

Develop your own performance evaluation form based on the skills required in each job.

Meet with each employee to review ratings and set objectives for the future.

BACKGROUND

Performance evaluations are important to employers as well as employees. They provide feedback for employees on their progress toward meeting goals and objectives that contribute to the aggregate growth and profit of the organization. The objective should be to help employees be successful in their jobs, so both they and the organization reap the rewards of success.

EXAMPLES

As the performance evaluation covers a relatively long period of time—usually the prior 3, 6, or 12 months—it is important that evaluators keep notes on their employees's performance during that whole period. In this way, the evaluation is more likely to accurately reflect an evaluation of the entire time period rather than just the most recent few weeks. This is even more important when the evaluator supervises several employees.

> [*Performance evaluations*] *provide feedback to employees on their progress toward meeting goals and objectives that contribute to the . . . growth and profit of the organization.*

It is at your discretion as a manager that you document any favorable or unfavorable employee performance or behavior. If an employee has done a meritorious job, you may choose to write a commendation. Similarly, if a negative incident comes to your attention, it is your choice to write it up. You *must*, however, be consistent in your treatment of similar infractions!

In either case, certain information should be included:

- Identify the performance and its result.
- State why such behavior is positive or negative.

- Mention specific dates of significant events of the performance, dates of previous commendations or warnings, and meetings with the employee about the same behavior.
- Include all pertinent facts.
- Be clear and concise.

If the documentation is for poor performance or nuisance behavior, you should also:

- Be specific in your expectations of what the employee is to do to correct the performance.
- Set target dates for completion of these goals.
- Mention the consequences of not taking action on these goals.
- End on a positive note, expressing confidence in the employee's ability to rectify the situation.

Finally, you should sign and date the documentation. In your meeting with the employee, request that the employee sign the documentation to signify receiving it. You may need to send the documentation certified mail with return receipt requested to have a signature on record. Put the documentation in the employee's personnel file.

The first level of documentation is verbal, to be documented it must be noted in some fashion. The second level of documentation is a written warning. Written warnings should follow verbal warnings.

The evaluator's notes, along with letters received from other managers and from customers or clients and samples of the employee's work, should be used in completing a performance evaluation form.

It is appropriate to attach the supporting documents, such as records of complaints or compliments, that help detail your ratings.

SUGGESTIONS

The first step to a successful performance evaluation is establishing clear, concise, and realistic performance objectives, which is critical for the employee to know how to meet your standards. Performance objectives should be established in the job description, so the employee knows what the employer expects from him before he even starts the job.

Well-written performance objectives have four characteristics:

1. *Results oriented.* Identifies a specific end product—an outcome.
2. *Measurable.* States how much, how many, and how well.
3. *Timebound.* Makes a specific time commitment.
4. *Specific plans.* Sets out the methods to accomplish the objective.

This is an example of a well-written objective: Learn and use the computer program for collections with greater than 90 percent accuracy by March 15 by training with the department manager two hours each day for one week.

When it comes time to actually do the evaluation, performance evaluation forms help to simplify and standardize the process. I recommend designing your own based on the skills required in each job category. The following list of skills is typical:

Quantity of work: Completes all assigned work in a timely manner. Utilizes time well.

Quality of work: Work is accurate, thorough, well organized, and effective.

Work habits: Gives care to equipment, materials, and supplies. Effective in the organization of work and the management of time. Establishes priorities.

Technical ability: Demonstrates the skill, knowledge, good judgment, and proficiency required to perform the job.

Human relations: Capable of obtaining cooperation and achieving results with and through others. Treats co-workers and general public with respect and courtesy.

Communication: Listens to others. Keeps co-workers informed. Produces clear, concise, and effective oral and written communication.

Responsibility: Follows instructions, rules, and procedures. Acts in a responsible and reliable manner.

Initiative: When appropriate, makes suggestions and takes independent action to solve problems and accomplish tasks.

Adaptability: Adjusts to changes and is not resistant to new routines, methods, or assignments.

Attendance: Tardiness held to a minimum and with good cause. No unexcused absences or excessive absenteeism.

Supervision: Effective in planning and controlling work activities of subordinates.

Each skill, if applicable to the job, should be rated. Typical rating categories are:

- Outstanding—Performance of the skill consistently and substantially exceeds the expected standards; is expert and highly competent.
- Commendable—Performance frequently exceeds the expected standards; is capable and competent.
- Satisfactory—Performance meets the expected standards; is adequate and acceptable.
- Needs improvement—Meets some of the requirements, but not all.
- Unacceptable—Fails to meet most of the requirements; performance is seriously deficient.

It is important to evaluate the importance of each skill to the job. Some skills are critically important to the job; others are less so. It is also important to provide a commentary with the rating. This gives you the opportunity to cite examples of the behaviors that contributed to your rating. This helps to communicate to the employee the basis of your rating and provides information to the employee on how to improve performance.

The performance evaluation form should also have an overall performance rating that is a summary of all the ratings, comments, and attachments.

The final part of a successful performance evaluation program is the meeting with the employee during which you go over your rating and set the performance objectives for the future. There are some basic steps to help make this meeting go smoothly and productively:

1. *Plan the meeting.* Plan what you want to say, what material you want to cover, and try to anticipate the possible reactions the employee might have. Arrange to be undisturbed.

2. *Have the facts.* Make sure the facts are from reliable and credible sources. Have specific and concrete examples of the behavior you wish to commend or correct. To change an employee's behavior, you must first be able to tell the employee exactly what the inappropriate behavior was and why it was inappropriate. If possible have examples of the work so you can go over errors together.

3. *Focus on the behavior, not the personality of the employee.* Deal with the performance problem, which can be changed, not character traits.

4. *Maintain the employee's self-esteem.* Detail the problem by focusing on the behavior. Keep the discussion positive. Avoid threats.

5. *Refer to previous discussions.* If you have had previous discussions with the employee on a problem, refer to those previous discussions.

6. *Stay calm.* You are in control. There is no need for you to get angry even if the employee does. Stand firm, talk about the performance that needs to be corrected.

7. *Explain performance objectives fully.* Tell employees exactly what is expected of them. Outline what resources the employee can use to achieve the desired results.

8. *Clearly state the specific time frame for each performance objective.*

9. *Ask for questions or if any points need clarification.*

10. *End on a positive note.* Thank the employee for past contributions. Assure employees of their capabilities to correct problems.

11. *Have the employee sign the performance evaluation form.* Explain that a signature does not indicate agreement, only that the evaluation has been discussed. If the employee refuses to sign, simply note that on the form.

A performance evaluation program carried out on a regular basis helps all employees to improve job performance. Improved job performance is in the best interest of the employee as well as the employer.

FOR MORE INFORMATION

Here's one source:

Cox, W N. *How to Prepare a Personnel Policy Manual.* Holland, MI: C R & Associates, 1989.

22. AIDS in the Workplace

Problem:

How do I help my employees deal with an HIV-positive employee?

Answers:

Provide reasonable accommodations as you would for employees with any life-threatening illness.

Review your company health plan to insure adequate coverage for all employees.

Establish an AIDS educational program.

BACKGROUND

I remember the day my secretary told me he had tested positive for the AIDS (acquired immune deficiency syndrome) virus. Suddenly I had to deal with HIV (human immunodeficiency virus) and AIDS in my office. I can't tell you what to do, but I can tell you the answers I uncovered for the questions I asked myself.

My secretary faces the chance of becoming a person with AIDS or a PWA—a label adopted by people with AIDS themselves. In 1982, a homosexual man with AIDS had a 30 percent chance of living for 18 months. Doctors had no idea what was causing the disease and only a vague idea of how it was spread.

> . . . *there is no known risk of transmitting the AIDS virus in the workplace.*

By 1987, the odds had changed to a 60 percent chance—and doctors now knew its cause. More than a hundred drugs had been tested for treating AIDS. The first drug approved by the US Food & Drug Administration for use against the AIDS virus was AZT. While it can prolong the lives of people with AIDS, it does not cure the disease.

As of May 1987, almost 36,000 AIDS cases had been reported with almost 21,000 deaths. In March 1989, the American College Health Association released the results of their study of blood samples taken from students on 20 US campuses. The results showed that 3 out of every 1,000 students are infected with the virus.

New drugs offer hope for the thousands of people with AIDS. Three drugs had been approved by the Food and Drug Administration (FDA) by the summer of 1989 to treat AIDS-related conditions. Of these three, aerosol pentamidine prevents a form of pneumonia that kills about 60 percent of people with AIDS. When announcing the new drug ganciclovir for the treatment of eye infections, FDA

Commissioner Frank Young said, "The face of AIDS is changing. By effectively combating opportunistic infections that accompany AIDS, medicine can now extend and improve the quality of life of individuals who are suffering with AIDS, even though there is no definite cure.[1]"

And in August 1989, Dr. Louis W Sullivan, the US secretary of Health and Human Services, called AIDS a "treatable" disease.[2]

By October 1990, doctors were predicting "normal" lives: "A patient with HIV will be treated similarly to a patient with diabetes and hypertension—prevent the progression of disease and maintain the quality of life," said Dr. Douglas Richman, an AIDS specialist at the University of California, San Diego.[3]

EXAMPLES

The current HIV tests show if the body has developed antibodies to the AIDS virus. Scientists have long known that the antibodies may not be detected for months or years after an infection. As former US Surgeon General C Everett Koop stated, "Many who test negatively might actually be positive due to recent exposure to the AIDS virus.[4]" So, the tests are of little value in determining HIV status at the time of testing. That is, they may not yet reveal an infection.

The US Department of Labor reported that in 1988 nearly four million job applicants and nearly one million workers were tested for drugs. More and more employers have required both job applicants and existing employees to submit urine and blood samples for drug and sometimes AIDS testing.

Workers have argued that the tests can be inaccurate and that positive test results do not themselves reflect impaired job performance. In June 1988, the National Labor Relations Board (NLRB) ruled that private employers cannot unilaterally

begin testing union workers for drug and alcohol use because testing is an issue that falls under collective bargaining
and must be part of union-management negotiations. And
in earlier court decisions, employees won protection from
surprise drug testing unless there is evidence of a problem
or they hold high-risk jobs. For now, however, neither the
courts nor the NLRB is discouraging the testing of job
applicants.

Those companies attempting to test for the AIDS virus as
a criterion for employment will face legal opposition. An
HIV infection does not, in and of itself, reflect a person's job
performance. Companies that test must make that policy
clearly understood by job applicants. Only with the guidance of medical and legal counsel should testing be implemented. Strict guidelines for confidentiality and fairness
must be adhered to.

However, by mid-1989 the San Francisco AIDS Foundation and other organizations providing AIDS services begin
endorsing widespread *voluntary* testing for the virus because new drugs can now prolong life if the virus is detected
early.

All things considered, testing is a personal decision—not
one for the company to make for individuals. As the National Academy of Sciences stated, "The decision of whether
to be tested for antibody to HIV should remain a matter for
individual discretion.[5]" But individuals should be informed
that testing can prolong lives.

With only the remotely possible exception of health care
and public safety professions, there is no known risk of
transmitting the AIDS virus in the workplace. Unlike mea-
sles or chicken pox, AIDS is not transmitted through casual
social contact. No special precautions are necessary, nor are
any job-site modifications in order. No cases of AIDS have
ever been linked to sharing work stations, telephones, water
fountains, coffee pots, eating facilities, or bathrooms. The
Occupational Safety and Health Administration (OSHA)

does not require employers to notify co-workers of an infected employee.

The policy at NYNEX Corporation states: "Employees who have contracted AIDS will not be prohibited from remaining in or returning to their normal workplace . . . there will be no restriction as to usage of common facilities nor any isolation of the employee from others.[6]"

What if other employees discover a co-worker is HIV positive and refuse to work on the basis that it is unsafe? GTE's policy can serve as a model. It reads: "If an employee refuses to work with or service establishments/home with AIDS victims, the employee should be counseled and educated. If the employee persists, he/she can be disciplined as in the case of any other unwarranted refusal to perform assigned work.[7]"

Thousands of people with AIDS are successfully employed. They need only the same concern and support you would want if you had a serious illness. You should plan for the possibility of more absences when the employee does not feel able to work.

The policy at General Dynamics states: "AIDS is considered a medical condition. If an employee can medically (physically) perform the job, he/she will continue as an active employee.[8]" And the policy at Dupont states: "An employee with a suspected or confirmed diagnosis of AIDS should be treated like any other employee with an illness.[9]"

SUGGESTIONS

In almost all cases, employees with AIDS are viewed as having a disability protected under the Federal Rehabilitation Act. In August 1989, President George Bush endorsed the Americans with Disabilities Act that would extend civil rights laws to 37 million Americans with some form of disability. The measure would include those with AIDS or those who are infected with HIV. The measure first applies to businesses with 25 or more employees; later it would include businesses with 15 or more employees.

'The AIDS virus does not discriminate by gender, race, or religion . . .'

Employees with AIDS should be treated like other employees with life-threatening illnesses, such as cancer or heart disease. Reasonable accommodations should be provided, just as for other life-threatening illnesses.

The policy at National Medical Enterprises states: "The availability of reasonable accommodations for an employee or applicant with AIDS must be considered . . . Depending on the particular circumstances, reasonable accommodation may include . . . modifying job duties, making reassignment or transfers [or] offering part-time or modified work schedules.[10]"

It's a fact of business life that the cost of employee health insurance has risen dramatically. It's also a fact that the cost of AIDS care was overestimated since people with AIDS are not currently hospitalized as often. Other health care costs have contributed more to the increased cost of health insurance.[11]

You should review your business's health and benefit package. Does your current carrier provide adequate coverage? If not, find a more comprehensive carrier. It may cost more, but all your employees need this protection.

The policy at Citicorp/Citibank states: "Staff known to have the AIDS virus . . . are entitled to the full range of policies, benefits, working conditions, courtesies, and amenities afforded to all staff.[12]" And the policy at Quaker Oats states: "AIDS is covered under our medical benefit plans just as any other disability or illness. There is no exclusion for AIDS as a pre-existing condition under Quaker's medical insurance.[13]"

The growing number of infected people and the still-prevalent misconceptions about the disease require businesses to implement comprehensive education efforts. An AIDS educational program should include the following:

1. *Posters and brochures.* Informative, accurate brochures are available from the US Public Health Service Centers for Disease Control and your state department of health. See telephone number below.

2. *Videos.* There are several nationally distributed videotapes that provide information on AIDS in the workplace. For example, the San Francisco AIDS foundation provides a 24-minute videotape and manual titled *The Next Step: HIV in the 90s* developed with the backing of several major corporations, including Pacific Bell and Bank of America.

3. *Speakers.* Contact local public health agencies or local AIDS projects for informed speakers.

The objective of your educational program should be to protect the health and dignity of all employees. The policy at Westinghouse states: "Westinghouse views AIDS as an illness, not as a crime or a punishment. We encourage compassion for the victims, and the provision of accurate appropriate information to all employees as an antidote to ungrounded fears or unreasonable exaggerations . . . [14]"

One common exaggeration has been the assumption that all homosexual men are promiscuous or have AIDS. Homosexual men did not cause AIDS. AIDS is a biological occurrence—not a moral punishment. There is no medical or ethical justification for avoiding contact with homosexual men.

The policy at Transamerica Life Companies states: "The AIDS virus does not discriminate by gender, race, or religion . . . we will *not* discriminate against any employee with this condition.[15]"

Every business and organization should be dealing directly and constructively with AIDS in the workplace now. My secretary? He's doing well—and he's the best secretary I've ever worked with.

FOR MORE INFORMATION

"AIDS, Civil Rights and the Public Health: America's Leaders Speak Out," San Francisco and Los Angeles, CA: National Gay Rights Advocates, 1988.

CDC National AIDS Hotline (24 hours, daily). 800-342-AIDS

Your state's department of health.

23. Empowering Employees

Problem:

How can I get my employees to take on more responsibility?

Answers:

Make your organization more entrepreneurial by maintaining goal-setting authority but surrendering some procedural authority to employees.

Recognize that democratizing an organization requires new skills of coalition and support building.

BACKGROUND

Over the past 50 years, most managers have relied on clearly defined jobs, tight controls, and supervision to reach their productivity goals. Today more and more managers are asking employees to take personal responsibility for their organizations. This change is the move from bureaucratic organizations to organizations that encourage and support entrepreneurial employees. Entrepreneurial employees are political in a positive way—and that is what is meant by *empowered employees.*

. . . *entrepreneurial organizations require new skills.*

Peter Block's book, *Flawless Consulting,* is about functioning in a staff capacity with maximum impact.[1] That book became the basis for the Block-Petrella-Weisbord's staff consulting skills workshops. Block's newest book, *The Empowered Manager,* is written for top- and mid-level line executives.[2]

EXAMPLES

Block believes bureaucracies have four core elements that guide employee behavior:

1. *Submission to authority.* Everyone has a boss. While managers get the illusion of power and influence from being bosses, employees get a feeling of helplessness that results in not accepting any responsibility—particularly when things go wrong.

2. *Denial of self-expression.* We spend most of our lives at our jobs and we all feel deeply about what happens there. But by discouraging employees from expressing their feelings, managers decrease employees' motivation and energy.

3. *Sacrifice for unnamed future rewards.* Bureaucracies demand employees do things that, if left to their own devices, they would choose not to do. Bureaucracies have gained this employee compliance by vague promises of job security. But today's fast-changing world makes these promises tenuous at best.

Bureaucracies require a pyramidal organization to maintain order and control. This is based on the pessimistic belief that employees cannot act responsibly on their own. It is based on the belief that strong, clear leadership from above telling employees how to operate is what makes an organization successful. It is based on the belief that we want only one platoon leader or one coach. But the evidence clearly shows that, today, high-control, autocratic, top-down systems are often less effective and less productive than more democratic participative systems.

Block describes the skills needed to be politically successful in traditional bureaucratic organizations:

- Manipulating situations and, at times, people.
- Managing information and plans carefully to our own advantage.
- Invoking the names of high-level people when seeking support for our projects.
- Becoming calculating in the way we manage relationships.
- Paying great attention to what people above us want from us.
- Living with the belief that in order to get ahead, we must be cautious in telling the truth.

These skills result from employees perceiving themselves to be in low-power positions. Block's thesis is that we give up too much power to the people around and above us in bureaucratic organizations. Our fear that power will be used against us in a destructive way leads us to be indirect and manipulative.

SUGGESTIONS

On the other hand, the entrepreneurial organization is based on an optimistic view of human nature: employees can take responsibility.

Rather than the manipulative skills common to bureaucracies, entrepreneurial organizations require new skills:

1. *Saying no when we mean no.* No longer do we hedge our positions out of fear of being disapproved of. No more "touching base" or "further study" when we really mean no.

2. *Sharing as much information as possible.* Let people know about budgets, plans, ideas, changes (and bad news) as soon as possible.

3. *Using language that describes reality.* Not only do we share as much information as possible, we share it in a way that the message gets through.

4. *Avoiding repositioning for the sake of acceptance.* Tying our project to the coattails of what is "hot" hurts our credibility. Tell people exactly what they're getting.

Block frequently uses the concept of political skills in entrepreneurial organizations. By that, he means coalition and support-building. He identifies *agreement* and *trust* as the two dimensions we need to assess and address with the people we attempt to influence.

High Agreement and High Trust (Allies)

Allies share our vision, and our trust in allies is great. The strategy is to share positive—and negative—information with them on a frequent and regular basis.

High Trust but Low Agreement (Opponents)

Block defines opponents as people whom we trust but with whom we honestly disagree. We should use opponents whom we trust to test the soundness of our positions. The strategy is to reaffirm our relationship based on trust, state our position, state our understanding of their position, and then engage in some kind of open problem solving.

High Agreement but Low Trust (Bedfellows)

People who agree with us, but in whom we have little or no trust, Block identifies as bedfellows. The strategy here is to reaffirm our agreement but openly acknowledge the caution that exists and then be clear about what you each want and how you're going to work together.

Low Trust and Unknown Agreement (Fence-Sitters)

The fence-sitter listens politely but simply will not take a stand for or against us. The strategy here is to smoke them out. State your position, ask where they stand, apply gentle pressure and encourage the fence-sitter to let us know what it would take for them to give us support. Block contends fence-sitters are not worth a great deal of energy. They will take a position when they think it is safe to do so.

Low Agreement and Low Trust (Adversaries)

Block defines people as adversaries only when all our attempts at negotiating an agreement and negotiating trust have failed. In that event, he recommends letting go. Stop trying to persuade them and stop doing anything to undermine or destroy them. Our strategy is now to reduce tension by eliminating contact and to reduce threat by letting the adversaries know we do understand their position.

Overall, our goal is to increase trust and agreement. Our strategies are to spend time with allies and to seek out new allies, then spend time with opponents we trust to sharpen our thinking. Next to be addressed are bedfellows who require frequent contact to maintain a fragile level of trust. As for adversaries, try to negotiate trust or agreement one more time and then say good bye.

. . . top-down systems are often less effective and less productive than more democratic participative systems.

Block maintains that to transform organizations into places where positive politics are the norm, we need to create a new contract between the employee and the organization. This can be done by doing the following:

- *Be your own authority.* We must ask employees to take responsibility for their own actions and their own department and to create an organization of their own choosing. Employees are the ultimate source of authority on what action will best serve the organization. Top management does give up some control but not the responsibility to establish and communicate organizational values and goals.
- *Encourage self-expression.* The entrepreneurial organization encourages employees to put passion, energy, excitement, and motivation back into their work.
- *Make commitments.* Demand commitment instead of sacrifice. Ask that employees take responsibility for their actions.

What are the origins of Block's thesis of empowerment? Its roots can be traced to the social consciousness of the 1960s according to Professor Karen Davidson, chair of management and business at the University of Redlands's Whitehead

Center for Lifelong Learning. As a society, we grew to accept all our fellow citizens as equals. Now we are ready to accept all our employees as equals. Treating others as equals means that we attempt to influence them in different ways than we did in the past.

When and where do you begin to make changes in your organization? Block says you begin today with your own "room." You start with what you can. Inmates really do run the prison.

FOR MORE INFORMATION

You'll want to consult the original reference:

Block, P. *The Empowered Manager: Positive Political Skills at Work.* San Francisco, CA: Jossey-Bass, 1987.

24. Terminating an Employee

Problem:

What's the best way to let an employee go?

Answers:

Follow proper procedure, using progressive discipline or negotiate a mutual agreement.

Explain the situation and settle issues in the exit interview.

BACKGROUND

Firing an employee is as critical a decision, if not more so, as hiring an employee. Most managers tell me they feel more confident and much more comfortable hiring than firing. To fire an employee today, you need to understand a bit of both law and psychology.

Centuries ago in Western history, employees could only leave their employment on their employer's terms. English common law changed that with the *employment at-will* doctrine. To equalize the relationship between employees and employers, employees could then quit—or employers could fire an employee—for any reason. Upon termination of employment neither party had any rights against the other.

Over time, though, employment at-will became a way for employers to keep the upper hand. With employees dependent upon the employer for jobs, employment at-will became the ultimate tool for maintaining a disciplined workforce.

Beginning early in the twentieth century, various state and federal laws were enacted that restricted employers's rights to terminate at-will. Violations could expose the employer to lawsuits. The 1990s saw a trend back to acceptance of the employment at-will concept.

EXAMPLES

Generally speaking, though, the following remain prohibited reasons for termination:

- Retaliation for applying for workers' compensation.
- Union activities.
- Race.
- Creed.

- Color.
- Sex.
- National origin.
- Vietnam veteran status.
- Disabled.
- Pregnancy.

Written employment contracts include both individual contracts for personal services and collective bargaining agreements. Employees covered by either of these are not considered to be employed at-will and may then only be terminated in accordance with the written agreement.

Most employment contracts require that *just cause* exist when an employee is terminated. Broadly defined, just cause means that the employee is at fault and that the employee's conduct is willfully at odds with reasonable expectations.

Just cause also requires employers to use reasonable judgment and to treat all employees uniformly and in a nonarbitrary and nondiscriminatory manner.

The basic question is whether proper procedures are followed. If not, the employer has erred. One recent survey showed that arbitrators reversed over 80 percent of dismissal cases because management had not followed proper procedure.

Problems with employees are usually either discipline problems or performance problems. Discipline problems are most commonly absenteeism and tardiness. Performance problems refer to the employee's failure to meet job standards.

Before you decide to fire an employee with discipline or performance problems, you should follow a policy of progressive discipline. Progressive discipline should be directed to correcting a situation—not to punishing the employee. Progressive discipline addresses the just cause issue of fair and equitable treatment. As such, it is the employer's best protection against grievances and lawsuits.

Progressive discipline is simply good management. We should tell employees as soon as a problem arises. Not to do so creates the false impression that no problem exists. Waiting for an annual review allows a problem to continue unaddressed for months, to the detriment of both the employer and the employee.

SUGGESTIONS

Generally, the following progressive discipline steps are considered appropriate:

1. *Oral reprimand.* Don't wait. Let the employee know immediately what the problem is. Note the date, time, and location.

2. *Counseling.* Later, explain to the employee how to improve. Describe what is expected and suggest ways that the employee can correct the problem. Note the date, time, and location of this meeting as well.

3. *Written warning(s).* Be specific. Define what the employee is doing wrong. Avoid indefinable terms, such as *bad attitude.* Use specifics, such as, late 20 minutes on each of three occasions in the past two-week period.

Specify a time by which the problem should be corrected and how you will determine if the problem has been corrected. Don't say, stop being late; say, expect no late check-ins as shown by time cards over the next two pay periods.

Finally, specify what the consequences of not correcting the problem will be.

4. *Hearing.* It is appropriate to give employees the opportunity to present their side of the problem. You may discover ways to correct the problem.

5. *Suspension.* This is a clear notice that the problem has not been addressed.

6. *Termination.* If the previous steps have been taken, the employee should not be surprised by termination.

7. *Exit interview.* Explain the reason for termination. Again, note date, time, and location of meeting.

Most white collar and managerial terminations are due to conflicts in attitudes, values, and temperaments rather than to discipline or performance problems.

Most skilled managers recognize that white collar and managerial terminations are a questionable practice. The dollar costs of severance and the recruiting and training of a replacement are high. In addition, the possibility of litigation and bad feelings among colleagues is great. Reassignment, relocation, and job outplacement are better options.

Other white-collar and managerial terminations may result from acquisitions and mergers, retrenchment and bankruptcy, or relocation and reorganization.

Rather than a termination in these and other cases, many managers recommend the use of a mutual agreement. These written agreements of a parting of the ways spell out the terms of the arrangement and the subsequent responsibilities of both parties. Because this procedure avoids an official termination, the manager can keep professional friends and enhance the company's reputation.

If termination is necessary, though, the manager should explain the situation to the employee and explain that management has decided to release the employee. Then, it is critical to turn the situation around quickly to a positive one. You should discuss the following:

1. First allow the employee to react and listen to his reactions.
2. Explain the company's policies on separation settlement.

3. Highlight the employee's positive attributes and strengths in finding other employment.
4. Offer whatever services the company has for outplacement.
5. Agree on what will be said to prospective new employers.

Termination can cause as much stress as divorce or the death of a loved one. People feel devastated by being fired. Being fired forces change, and that change is a source of both stress and opportunity. Termination forces a review of life goals, career expectations, and personal and professional goals.

At one time, I worked with terminated faculty at a New York college. I recall the time and sheer agony managers put into those decisions, trying their best to avoid the terminations. I also recall the anxiety of the employees who knew they might be terminated. I was struck, however, that in all cases that actually resulted in termination, the employees secured better jobs somewhere else and felt better about themselves and their new jobs.

The terminated employee should understand that termination is an opportunity to do better. The immediate shock will pass. New and rewarding challenges lie ahead in a different environment.

FOR MORE INFORMATION

You'll find several books in the business section to help you. Here's one:

Bequai, A. *Every Manager's Legal Guide to Firing.* Homewood, IL: Business One Irwin, 1991.

Endnotes

Question 1:

[1] L L Barker, *Listening Behavior* (Englewood Cliffs, NJ: Prentice-Hall, 1971).

Question 2:

[1] M Doyle and D Straus, *How to Make Meetings Work* (New York, NY: Wyden Books, 1976).

Question 3:

[1] G W Allport and L Postman, *The Psychology of Rumor* (New York, NY: Russell & Russell, 1965).

[2] F E Jandt and C D Beaver, "A Pilot Study on Alienation and Anxiety During a Rumored Plant Closing," *Journal of Applied Communications Research* vol. 1, 1973, pp. 105–114.

[3] K Davis, *Human Behavior at Work* (New York, NY: McGraw-Hill, 1972).

Question 4:

[1] W C Redding, "Position Paper: A Response to Discussions at the Ad Hoc Conference on Organizational Communication," in *Organizational Communication,* 4th ed, ed. G M Goldhaber (Dubuque, IA: William C Brown Publishers, 1986), p. 25.

[2] Davis, *op. cit.*

[3] E Planty and W Machaver, "Upward Communications: A Project in Executive Development," *Personnel,* January 1952, pp. 304–318.

Question 5:

[1] K H Blanchard and S Johnson, *The One Minute Manager* (New York NY: Morrow, 1982).

Question 9:

[1] R A MacKenzie, *The Time Trap*. New York, NY: Amacom, 1990.

[2] R A MacKenzie, "How to Make the Most of Your Time," *U.S. News and World Report*, vol. 75, December 3, 1973, pp. 45–48ff.

Question 11:

[1] R Von Oech, *A Whack on the Side of the Head* (New York, NY: Warner Books, 1983).

[2] H A Hornstein, *Managerial Courage: Revitalizing Your Company Without Sacrificing Your Job* (New York, NY: John Wiley & Sons, 1986).

Question 14:

[1] *USA Weekend*, October 16, 1988.

[2] J W Gardner, *On Leadership* (New York, NY: Free Press, 1990).

Question 15:

[1] *New York Times*, 21, April 1989, Section I.

[2] Independent Gallup Polls (Wilmington, DE: Scholarly Resources, 1989).

[3] A Etzioni, "Is Corporate Crime Worth the Time?" *Business & Society Review*, vol. 73, Spring 1990, pp. 32–35.

Question 16:

[1] M J Dooher and E Marting, eds., *Selection of Management Personnel* (New York, NY: American Management Association, 1957).

Question 18:

[1] I L Janis, *Victims of Groupthink* (Boston, MA: Houghton Mifflin, 1972).

Question 19:

[1] US Bureau of the Census, *Statistical Abstract of the United States* (Washington, DC various editions).

Question 20:

[1] Independent Gallup Polls (Wilmington, DE: Scholarly Resources).

[2] Independent Gallup Polls (Wilmington, DE: Scholarly Resources).

[3] A Brisolara, *The Alcoholic Employee* (New York, NY: Human Sciences Press, 1979).

[4] R M Weiss, *Dealing with Alcoholism in the Workplace* (New York, NY: Conference Board, 1980).

Question 22:

[1] As cited in *AIDS, Civil Rights and the Public Health: America's Leaders Speak Out.*

[2] ibid.

[3] ibid.

[4] ibid.

[5] ibid.

[6] ibid.

[7] ibid.

[8] ibid.

[9] ibid.

[10] ibid.

[11] ibid.

[12] ibid.

[13] ibid.

[14] ibid.

[15] ibid.

Question 23:

[1] P Block, *Flawless Consulting: A Guide to Getting Your Expertise Used* (San Diego, CA: University Associates, 1981).

[2] P Block, *The Empowered Manager: Positive Political Skills at Work* (San Francisco, CA: Jossey-Bass, 1987).

Index

Other excellent resources available from Irwin Professional Publishing . . .

Women in the Workplace Eliminating Sexual Harassment and Improving Cross-Gender Communication
Module II
Participant's Guide
(32 pages, paper)
ISBN 1–55623–826–6
Packs of 10 ISBN
0–7863–0176–7
Leader's Guide
(75 pages, 3-ring binder)
ISBN 0–7863–0161–9

Cultural Diversity Challenges and Opportunities
Module III
Participant's Workbook
(32 pages, paper)
ISBN 1–55623–827–4

Packs of 10 ISBN
0–7863–0173–2
Leader's Guide
(75 pages, 3-ring binder)
ISBN 0–7863–0159–7

Bridging the Age Gap
Module IV
Participant's Workbook
(32 pages, paper)
ISBN 1–55623–828–2
Packs of 10 ISBN
–7863–0174–0
Leader's Guide
(75 pages, 3-ring binder)
ISBN 0–7863–0160–0

Available at fine bookstores and libraries everywhere.

BUSINESS REPLY MAIL

FIRST CLASS   PERMIT NO. 99   HOMEWOOD, IL

POSTAGE WILL BE PAID BY ADDRESSEE

IRWIN

Professional Publishing

Attn: Cindy Zigmund
1333 Burr Ridge Parkway
Burr Ridge, IL 60521-0081

1. How did you find out about this Briefcase Book?

☐ Bookstore   ☐ Irwin Catalog
☐ Advertisement   ☐ Convention
☐ Flyer   ☐ Other Catalog
☐ Sales Rep

other _____

2. Was this book provided by your organization or did you purchase this book for yourself?

☐ individual purchase
☐ organizational purchase

3. Are you using this book as a part of a training program?

☐ yes   ☐ no

4. Did this book meet your expectations?

☐ yes   ☐ no

(please explain)

_____
_____
_____

5. What other topics would you like to see addressed in this series?

(Please list)

_____
_____
_____

6. ☐ Please have a sales representative call me.

I am interested in:

☐ bulk purchase discounts
☐ custom publishing

7. ☐ Please send me a catalog of your products.

Name _____

Title _____

Organization _____

Address _____

City, State, Zip _____

Phone _____